Scripture Therapy and Choice Theory

Bishop Les
and
Scripture Therapy Minister RoxAnne Triché

ISBN 978-1-64258-024-2 (paperback)
ISBN 978-1-64258-025-9 (digital)

Copyright © 2018 by Bishop Les and Scripture Therapy Minister RoxAnne Triché

All rights reserved. No part of this publication may be reproduced, distributed, or transmitted in any form or by any means, including photocopying, recording, or other electronic or mechanical methods without the prior written permission of the publisher. For permission requests, solicit the publisher via the address below.

Christian Faith Publishing, Inc.
832 Park Avenue
Meadville, PA 16335
www.christianfaithpublishing.com

Printed in the United States of America

Contents

Acknowledgments 5
Opening Prayer 7
Introduction 9

Chapter 1: Where We Begin 13
Chapter 2: Who Are You? 17
Chapter 3: The Foundation 22
Chapter 4: Choice Theory and Internal Empowerment 37
Chapter 5: Basic Needs 46
Chapter 6: SEEAL Assessment 65
Chapter 7: Your Quality World 77
Chapter 8: Aligning Your Quality World 84
Chapter 9: Total Behavior 90
Chapter 10: PRITTT Formula 97
Chapter 11: Giving Back and Mentoring 105
Chapter 12: Self-Change through Self-Evaluation 112
Chapter 13: Reflecting and Summary 118

Scripture Therapy 121

Acknowledgments

When I take the time to reflect on my life, I realize that there are only three types of persons that have been zealous about helping me attain what God has planned for me. The first is the Lord who is "my Shepherd, and I shall not want . . ." He is the beginning and end of all I aspire to do! Thank You, Jesus, for the strength, wisdom, power, and tenacity You gave me to pursue my God-given purpose, despite life's many challenges. Furthermore, thank you for allowing me to see You in all that I do to help others enhance their relationships, behavior, choices, and trust in You.

The second person committed to helping me in my life is my wife, RoxAnne Triché, whom God gave me to make me complete, to be the perfect fit for me, and to bring about the reality of God's "unorthodox math," which is *and they shall become one flesh . . .* (Genesis 2:24). Thank you, RoxAnne, for sticking with me through what appeared to be "a trip through hell," but in reality was a perfecting and equipping period in the Cave of Adullam designed to make me a better person. Thank you for helping me promote unity without bondage, facilitate internal empowerment and reformation, and build a legacy for others to follow.

The third group of people who help me through times of great challenge are those who know, understand, and strive to help bring clarity to the above. These are the people who serve as my personal board of directors. They guide, support, and pray for me. They also encourage me to stay focused and choose to find my happiness. Thank you,

- Dr. William Glasser and Carleen Glasser (Los Angeles, CA)
- Bishop Jeff Battle (Atlanta, GA)

- Bishop Larry Jordan (Upper Marlboro, MD)
- Bishop Herman and Pastor Patrice Tinsley (South Africa and San Dimas, CA)
- Episcopal Pastor John A. Cherry and Reverend Diana P. Cherry (Temple Hill, MD)
- Pastor Steve and Minister Debra Coleman (Moreno Valley, CA)
- Ministers Ed and Brenda Ballantine (Redding, CA)
- Ministers Otis and Donna Reedy (Menifee, CA)
- The John Maxwell Team (Orlando, FL)

Special thanks to the 2,500+ Choice Theory Connections—Internal Empowerment Coaching students at the California Institution for Women, and the 100 male students at Centinela State Prison. You showed me how to teach you "why and how you behave," and how to teach those whose primary languages are not English. You became my "ministry of restoring, reframing, and reallocating resources," teaching others to reorganize their lives.

I thank our first Orange County, California students, who tested our *Scripture Therapy* and Choice Theory (STACT) teaching materials in 2015 by sharing them with small focus groups. Because of their efforts, on Father's Day 2016, we started teaching our first STACT class at a California correctional institution. There were twenty-seven ethnic and generationally diverse students in attendance. Each student agreed to bring one additional person whom they felt would benefit from the teachings the Spirit of God would bring forward in future lessons. The growth of STACT since 2015 has been a blessing to facilitators, supporters, and students.

Thank you, you're all awesome!
God's blessings to you!

Opening Prayer

Father God, in that name that is above every name, that name in which every knee shall bow and every tongue shall confess that "Jesus is Lord," we come before You. Father, we thank You for the work that Jesus did before, during, and after His cross experience to redeem the world. We thank You, Father God, for the birth, death, and resurrection of Jesus the Christ. Thank You for the blood He shed for each of us and for the work He calls us to do, according to the Holy Spirit.

Father, bless the readers and students of our teachings and those You have ordained to share this book. Bless all the lessons that will come forth from our trials, tribulations, and challenges. Remove all that stands between us and the fulfillment of this assignment. Help us define relationships, behavior, choices, and trust in You to free Your people from bondage, trickery, and incomplete and incorrect teachings of Your Word and character.

Bless our minds and the minds of those You commissioned to assist us in publishing this book, to strategically teach and implement Your principles, practices, and procedures to help us guide and activate "the Mind of Christ" in the readers.

Now, Father God, we thank You for good health, for sound minds, and for prospering our students, the readers, and ourselves, according to Your Word. We set ourselves in agreement with You, Your Word, and Your Spirit, to acknowledge Matthew 28:18–20, which says,

> Jesus came and spoke to them [the Disciples], saying, "All authority has been given to Me in heaven and on earth.

therefore and make disciples of all the nations, baptizing them in the name of the Father and of the Son and of the Holy Spirit,

them to observe all things that I have commanded you; and lo, I am with you always, even to the end of the age." Amen.

We thank You and give You the glory, honor, and praise. We believe this prayer has been heard and answered by You, in the mighty name of Jesus, the Christ.

Amen.

Introduction

Greetings in the name of our Lord and Savior, Jesus! It is with full acknowledgment of the grace of God that I can pen this book. Without God, nothing is possible.

Writing to the purpose of God is not easy. However, writing begins to flow when we submit to the teachings and instructions of the Spirit of God. So, I submit myself to the Spirit of God, praying He will write through me and prepare the reader's heart to receive the seed and cultivate what the Lord will allow to emerge from reading this book.

Welcome to the evidence-supported Choice Theory Connections—Internal Empowerment Coaching Program (*Scripture Therapy*), approved by Loyola Marymount University. This program has been tailor-made for *you*! The program is focused toward those who choose to embark on addressing the world's number one challenge—doing what God called you to do and taking control of your life.

I am writing this book in response to a personal charge given by the Holy Spirit at a time when it seemed that the enemy targeted many of his demonic spirits, resources, and personal efforts to derail my desire to honor the calling God placed upon my life.

It seems that for many years, I experienced what the biblical character Job experienced, an attack by the enemy whose purpose is to kill, steal, and destroy.

These areas are essential components of the enemy's purpose. These actions are the enemy's ways of attempting to cause me to stop, detour, become derailed, and change priorities the Lord set for me.

So, in a way, this writing is my attempt to reaffirm and implement what I was called to do in the kingdom of God. That is to be led by the Spirit of God, to be a Godly example, ambassador, and point man for God, and to challenge the thinking and actions of individuals to activate the "mind of Christ" in them.

> 1 Corinthians 2:10–16
> The Spirit searches all things, even the deep things of God.
> For who among men knows the thoughts of a man except the man's spirit within him? In the same way no one knows the thoughts of God except the Spirit of God.
> We have not received the spirit of the world, but the Spirit who is from God, that we may understand what God has freely given us.
> This is what we speak, not in words taught us by human wisdom, but in words taught by the Spirit, expressing spiritual truths in spiritual words.
> The man without the Spirit does not accept the things that come from the Spirit of God, for they are foolishness to him, and he cannot understand them, because they are spiritually discerned.
> The spiritual man makes judgments about all things, but he himself is not subject to any man's judgment:
> For who has known the mind of the Lord that he may instruct him? But we have the mind of Christ.

As I look back on two decades of ministry leadership, I have been blessed in so many areas. I have consulted in ministries with memberships from thirty to thirty thousand such as Faith Missions International, Crenshaw Christian Center, the Los Angeles Dream Center, the City of Refuge, Abundant Living Family Church, From the Heart Church Ministries, and the Believers Worship Center. My ministry focus has been on church leadership and governance.

Although I primarily focused on Jesus, with a secondary focus on leadership and governance, in recent years, God anointed me to focus on relationships, behavior, choices, and trust issues for myself and others. There is still much work to be done! In fact, it is apparent that I failed to exercise opportunities to teach and preach the Word of God, hoping I could continue to handle governance and administrative matters.

Stated differently, I spent my time helping faith-based organizations launch visions, design organizational structures, review and audit educational programs, train ministry leaders, plant churches in the USA, South America, and other places abroad, write administrative policies and procedures, and conduct nationwide searches for executive pastors. However, I should have simultaneously preached and taught Jesus to a greater number of people.

Father God, I believe I should have spent more time preaching Jesus. Instead, I spent too much time being distracted by the enemy and his forces and allowing those closest to me to cause me to lose focus. I am now resubmitting to Your reformation, and preparing to write and teach about Jesus!

In the name of Jesus, I repent. Amen

Today, I am charged with using the character of God to minister the gospel of Jesus Christ, through Scripture. My instructions from God are to mentor others; to take an in-depth look at the life of Jesus and use Scripture to enhance individuals' relationships, behavior, choices, and trust to lead God's people from bondage, trickery, and incomplete and incorrect teachings to being free in the Lord and to teach about Jesus, facilitating empowerment of the Holy Spirit, and building legacies for others to follow.

Thank you for joining with me today as we follow our Lord and Savior Jesus Christ and pursue all He has for us.

Scripture Therapy is about helping you explore God's desire for your life.

Our vision. Hear the voice of God, follow His instructions, and teach *Scripture Therapy* and Choice Theory to the world.

Our mission. Guide individuals to trust God by studying and applying the Word of God and building legacies for others to follow.

Our method. Use the Holy Spirit's teaching and counseling to promote *Scripture Therapy* and Choice Theory as a vehicle to deliver God's teachings to

- create unity without bondage
- counsel individuals to activate the mind of Christ in them
- spread the Gospel of Jesus Christ to the world.

The Center for *Scripture Therapy* offers Scripture-based Internal Empowerment Coaching and Choice Theory teachings as the beginning of a *personal journey* to improve relationships, behavior, choices, trust, and the quality of life we desire with God and others.

CHAPTER 1

Where We Begin

Scripture Therapy was developed to meet a need within the Body of Christ for transformative counseling and teaching. It's based on the following principles and practices:

- The Word of God
- Yielding to reformation by the Spirit of God
- Internal Empowerment Coaching
- Scriptural application of Choice Theory and Reality Therapy

This book will help you self-assess and yield your life to reorganizing by the Holy Spirit. It will help you become more knowledgeable about the Word of God, enhance your relationships with God and others, and aid your spiritual and professional development. *Scripture Therapy* brings awareness of behaviors and choices that conflict with the pursuit of God in your life. As this awareness grows, you are empowered to gain effective control of your life which leads to:

*b*ecoming less reactive to peer pressure
*l*earning to restore, reframe and reallocate resources
*e*nhancing positive relationships
*s*etting effective goals and making responsible decisions
*s*haring your knowledge of *Scripture Therapy* with others

*e*valuating your level of obedience to God's instruction
*d*eveloping a Godly plan of action to fulfill God's purpose for your life

The changes in your life will impact your total behavior—your thinking, actions, feeling, and physiology. You will gain tools to create positive communications for living, working, education, and social interaction, and create a culture of giving back and mentoring others—positively influencing generations and inspiring a living legacy.

Scripture Therapy also uses the five basic needs of Choice Theory as developed by William Glasser MD (survival, love and belonging, power, freedom, and fun) to help you understand what you want most and how to obtain happiness and freedom. You will reflect on what God says about events that affect you, determine if they bring positive or negative input into your life, and consider why they are in your life. *You, along with God,* decide what issues you want to address, get rid of baggage weighing heavy on your mind, and learn the tricks of the enemy you have allowed in your life.

You will benefit from *Scripture Therapy* if you feel trapped, desire to reorganize your spiritual life, need clarity in your personal or professional life pursuits, want to understand your needs and why you do the things you do, are confronted with an abundance of life challenges, yearn to be trained professionally to fulfill your God-given call and assignments, or are not satisfied with your life choices and instead desire to chart Godly pathways to change.

The results of *Scripture Therapy* require the teachings and counseling of the Holy Spirit, God-ordained pruning processes, and personal obedience to the Word of God.

We begin and end based upon Scripture.

> Hebrews 4:12
> For the word of God *is* living and powerful, and sharper than any two-edged sword, piercing even to the division of soul and spirit, and of joints and marrow, and is a discerner of the thoughts and intents of the heart.

SCRIPTURE THERAPY AND CHOICE THEORY

The objectives of this book are focused on personal growth and change. This is different for everyone, but all of us can use the information and tools to experience positive life changes.

Objectives of *Scripture Therapy*:

1. You will learn to cultivate good relationships.

   Ecclesiastes 4:9–12
   Two *are* better than one, Because they have a good reward for their labor.
   　For if they fall, one will lift up his companion. But woe to him *who is* alone when he falls, For *he has* no one to help him up. Again, if two lie down together, they will keep warm; But how can one be warm *alone?*
   　Though one may be overpowered by another, two can withstand him. And a threefold cord is not quickly broken.

2. You will choose effective behavior.

   James 1:22
   But be doers of the word, and not hearers only, deceiving yourselves.

3. You will make life-changing choices.

   Deuteronomy 30:19
   I call heaven and earth as witnesses today against you, *that* I have set before you life and death, blessing and cursing; therefore choose life, that both you and your descendants may live.

The changes in your relationships, behaviors, choices, and trust in God are entirely within your control. *Scripture Therapy* is about taking responsibility for your life, yielding to the Spirit of God, getting into your Godly position, purpose, and place, activating the "mind of Christ" in you, demonstrating the character of God, learning how to make Godly decisions, developing God-ordained reformation plans, and implementing Internal Empowerment Coaching's principles.

May God bless you as you begin this journey.

CHAPTER 2

Who Are You?

STACT delves deep into self-reflection. This is necessary for personal growth. To start, learn to be aware of the thoughts you have about yourself. You may have quite a monologue taking place in your mind without even realizing it. These thoughts have a direct impact on your feelings, actions, and physiology. Many mental health challenges are transformed when people learn to consciously pay attention to their thoughts and change them to thoughts that are Godly, true, and useful.

As you are reading through this book, be sure to apply the things you learn and practice these new skills daily and mindfully.

Take some time to really think about yourself. Allow yourself to answer the following questions freely and without editing. Just write down what comes to your mind.

Who are you?

_____
_____
_____
_____
_____
_____

BISHOP LES AND SCRIPTURE THERAPY
MINISTER ROXANNE TRICHÉ

What thoughts do you have about yourself?

_____
_____
_____
_____
_____

Why are you reading this book?

_____
_____
_____
_____
_____

What's one unique characteristic, skill, or fact that only God knows about you?

_____
_____
_____
_____
_____

Pick a year God called and anointed you to do something. What was it and what did you do?

_____
_____
_____
_____
_____

SCRIPTURE THERAPY AND CHOICE THEORY

Are you running from God's calling on your life? If yes, why? If no, how are you answering God's calling on your life?

_____
_____
_____
_____
_____

Describe the relationship you aspire to have with God and explain why you want this.

_____
_____
_____
_____
_____

Has God given you a vision? If yes, explain what it is. If no, explain why you feel you do not have a vision from God.

_____
_____
_____
_____
_____

Next, take some time to think about who you are in these five key areas:

1. Your relationship with God
2. Your behavior toward the Word of God
3. Choices you are making between God and the enemy
4. Level of happiness you experienced today
5. Actions needed to receive what God has for you

BISHOP LES AND SCRIPTURE THERAPY
MINISTER ROXANNE TRICHÉ

Take these thoughts and use them to describe yourself in an acrostic of your first and last name. Here's an example of this exercise, using the names *God* and *Jesus*.

G = Gracious, good
O = Omniscient: knows all, omnipresent; is everywhere at once, omnipotent; all powerful
D = Divine, devoted

J = Just
E = Eternal; always was, always is, always will be
S = Savior of all who choose to believe
U = Universal for all people
S = Sovereign, seeker of all lost

Here's an example using the author's name.

L = Love the Word of God and its power
E = Elevating my gifts and talents to fulfill my purpose
S = Saved, serious, and a solid foundation for self and others

T = Trustworthy; fear God, inspire to keep his commandments
R = Refuse to work for the enemy
I = In submission to the Word of God
C = Christian, compassionate, and yielded to the Holy Spirit
H = Humble and honest in dealing with others
É = Eager to use my gifts and talents to help others

SCRIPTURE THERAPY AND CHOICE THEORY

Now you try!

___

Discuss what you learned about yourself from the exercise. Did anything surprise you?

___

The best thing about this exercise is that students can find Scriptures to support who they are! If they are having a challenging day, this exercise is a perfect way to change the "picture in their head." So naturally, the perspective on their day gets lifted up, or they could choose to stumble. The choice is theirs.

> 1 Peter 2:9
> But you *are* a chosen generation, a royal priesthood, a holy nation, His own special people, that you may proclaim the praises of Him who called you out of darkness into His marvelous light.

CHAPTER 3

The Foundation

Scripture Therapy is about *you* discovering *you* through the Word of God, Choice Theory, and Internal Empowerment coaching *instead* of being the person others want you to be. We need to be clear about Scripture since this is the basis for our journey.

Scripture is

1. speaking with divine authority; The Word of God, His character, and His plan for mankind
2. possessing the quality of foresight and the active power of preaching
3. standing for its Divine Author, with a warning that Scripture is *perpetual*:

    - always
    - eternal
    - forever
    - unending
    - ever living
    - continuous
    - everlasting as the *living voice of God*

    (*Vine's Expository Dictionary, Biblical Words* [Thomas Nelson, 1985], s.v. "perpetual")

SCRIPTURE THERAPY AND CHOICE THEORY

What does God say about Scripture?

> 2 Timothy 3:16–17
> All Scripture *is* given by inspiration of God, and *is* profitable for doctrine, for reproof, for correction, for instruction in righteousness, that the man of God may be complete, thoroughly equipped for every good work.

What else does God say about Scripture?

_____
_____
_____
_____
_____
_____

During our first course offering of *Scripture Therapy*, we asked our Orange County, California, students, "Why are you interested in taking this course?" Below are some of their responses:

- "Because I want to improve my life, based on the Word of God, and never stop growing, until the day I die" *(Fabiola)*.
- "As a believer of Christ, it is imperative, that I study God's Word in a simple, easy to understand way, so I can remember the Word of God and its daily application" *(Tiffani)*.
- "*Scripture Therapy* opens my whole outlook, and I can pick apart how I view things. Now I can work on myself, and be more open to what God has to say about how I live my life" *(Rick)*.

Now that you have read how other students answered the question, think about why you are interested in taking this course that uses Scripture as the foundational teaching.

_____
_____
_____
_____
_____
_____

Scripture is the Power of God—"I AM!" That's it, and that's all.

No one can add to or take away from the Word of God! The Power of God: His Word, His character, and His will.

How do you define the Power of God?

_____
_____
_____
_____
_____
_____

What has been your experience with the Power of God?

_____
_____
_____
_____
_____
_____

The Power of God is God, who is indescribable!

Let's discuss God, His Power, and how he is truly indescribable. What does that mean?

SCRIPTURE THERAPY AND CHOICE THEORY

Indescribable is:

- impossible to describe
- exceeding description
- beyond descriptive words, unspeakable, inexpressible, incommunicable
- and yet it begs a description!

Some of our most eloquent theologians, televangelists, preachers, and intercessors have found it impossible to describe the *Indescribable Gift*. I appeal to you to let the Holy Spirit—our Teacher—tell you about the *Indescribable Gift*. And when we describe the *Indescribable Gift*, we should just say, "That's God!"

Saying, "That's God!" recognizes God is *all*, and in *all*. It helps us to remember that we should express thanks, appreciation, and gratitude to God. It enables us to continue to use God's:

- mouth to *speak*
- legs to *walk*
- brain to *think*
- air to *breathe*
- hands to *hold* His Bible
- resources to *acquire* things within His will
- *His blessing* to *be a blessing* to ourselves and others.

The closest we can get to describing this *Indescribable Gift* (the Power of God) is through understanding the term *indispensable*. For the purpose of this writing, *indispensable* means "cannot be destroyed, thrown away, or changed."

Jesus is indispensable because He is our only INTERCESSOR.

Some of us have tried Buddha, Ouija boards, tarot readers, fortune-tellers, multiple religions, and all sorts of experts. *But* none of these things or people have access to God without Jesus, the *Intercessor*.

Try *your* arms. See if you can bring Salvation upon yourself and others. Then try to sustain yourself. You can't. We can't.

Jesus is indispensable because He is our only REMEDY.

- NO magic
- NO love potions
- NO Chinese herbs
- NO super vitamins
- NO experts can serve as the REMEDY

This assignment is only for Jesus!

Jesus is *our* Remedy. In Genesis, Adam went looking for the remedy in all the wrong places. He went looking for answers at the wrong tree—the tree of good and evil. Adam associated with the *wrong tree.*

Too many people are looking for "the answer" in man, his church, and the wrong tree when God has the answers in His Word:

- They look for *tree leaves* to smoke ("little weed to satisfy the need").
- They look for *tree vines* to make their wine.
- They look for *tree roots* to burn in their fireplace while sleeping with other people's partners, acquaintances, and sometimes both at the same time.

Daniel 4:20–23 tells the story of Daniel interpreting a dream for King Nebuchadnezzar regarding a tree. He says to the king,

> The tree that you saw, which grew and became strong, whose height reached to the heavens and which could be seen by all the earth, whose leaves were lovely and its fruit abundant, in which was food for all, under which the beasts of the field dwelt, and in whose branches the birds of the heaven had their home—it is you, O king, who have grown and become strong; for your great-

> ness has grown and reaches to the heavens, and your dominion to the end of the earth.
>
> And inasmuch as the king saw a watcher, a holy one, coming down from heaven saying, 'Chop down the tree and destroy it, but leave its stump and roots in the earth, bound with a band of iron and bronze in the tender grass of the field . . .

I believe God has been busy cutting down trees in the forest of communities. Some of us have allowed ourselves to be destroyed in different ways, *but* God is commanding *our stump* to remain steadfast, unmovable, and holding on until *God blesses us.*

So, Father God, we have left the STUMPS, *and we await Your revitalization plan, and we are asking for it this day!*

God always has plans for TREES:

- He caused Himself to go to the *tree* to redeem us.
- He allowed Himself to be nailed to a *tree.*

But

- He didn't stay on the tree—neither shall we.
- He no longer hangs on the tree—neither shall we.
- He now sits at the right hand of the Father as *our only* REMEDY.

Jesus is indispensable because He is our only NOURISHMENT.

Despite my Sunday morning prayers that remind me that God's sheep are hungry; despite our daily shopping at Wal-Mart, Albertson's, and Trader Joe's, the food we buy will *not* satisfy the appetite, thirst, or hunger.

God has assigned ministers to feed His sheep with His Food.

But as sheep,

- let's prepare to dine;
- let's prepare to digest, and gain nourishment, revelation, and Godly wisdom;
- let's prepare to activate the Word of God, first in our own hearts and behaviors; and
- let's prepare to be served by the Holy Spirit, through His vessels (His teachers, counselors, etc.).

My prayer is that we reject pride, guilt, unforgiveness, self-righteousness, and anything else the enemy attempts to put before us, and we ready ourselves for the meals God's vessels prepare from the "great book of recipe instructions," the Bible.

Some may need catastrophic events in their lives before they agree to be humbly fed the Word of God.

- They may speak horrible things that bring harmful consequences.
- They may see a loved one get hurt.
- They may experience a sudden loss of a job or loved one, physical abuse, extreme illness, loss of a major business account, or something else.

These events cause us to either cry out to God and repent or harden our hearts because of unmet expectations. Repenting (we turn around and change from partnering with Satan to a covenant relationship with Jesus) will cause us to seek and be fed the Word of God. To sit at His table—just to be around Him. Only He, Jesus Christ, is our refuge. Our Nourishment is provided by the Maker of spiritual food, Jesus. Our menu is prepared by the Holy Ghost, and all food served is washed in *the organic Blood of Jesus*!

SCRIPTURE THERAPY AND CHOICE THEORY

> John 6:35
> And Jesus said to them, "I am the bread of life. He who comes to Me shall never hunger, and he who believes in Me shall never thirst."

PRAISE THE LORD!

Jesus is indispensable because He is our only SOURCE of TRUTH.

> John 8:31–32
> Then Jesus said to those Jews who believed Him, "If you abide in My word, you are My disciples indeed.
> And you shall know the truth, and the truth shall make you free."

> 1 John 4:1
> Beloved, do not believe every spirit, but test the spirits, whether they are of God; because many false prophets have gone out into the world.

Our spiritual leaders may be appointed by God; however, they are only human. The Bible tells us to pray for our leaders and to watch and pray lest we fall. Leaders are under considerable opposition and temptation. Some are only in it for themselves and do not preach the truth.

There is danger in trying to change the Truth.

> Revelation 22:19
> And if anyone takes away from the words of the book of this prophecy, God shall take away his part from the Book of Life, from the holy city, and *from* the things which are written in this book.

BISHOP LES AND SCRIPTURE THERAPY
MINISTER ROXANNE TRICHÉ

If we follow Jesus, our *Source* of *Truth*, we will get blessed! We will get directions to *Truth* (Jesus) and we will get *Life* with *Truth* (Jesus). When our will starts lining up with His will, we will start to see things—the *truth* of things—the way Jesus sees them.

Jesus is indispensable because He is our only SAVIOR.

We have a choice: the King of kings or the lord of lies and flies. If we choose Jesus, we get blessed with both *Lord and Savior*. If we choose the lord of lies and flies, we are sharing the lie that we can lead ourselves to salvation, righteousness, and eternal life.

We didn't make this up—it's in the Scripture! If you don't believe us, try another name and wait for empty results.

We can try the president's name, Dr. Phil's name, our pastor's name, 50 Cent's name, Oprah's name, or for that matter our own name, but nothing will happen.

We can say other names, *but* Salvation comes only through Jesus. Jesus provided the blood for our redemption, foundation, cornerstone, blueprint, His character, and sound doctrine, for which we are to reorganize our lives and find happiness.

> Romans 10:9–10
> That if you confess with your mouth the Lord Jesus and believe in your heart that God has raised Him from the dead, you will be saved.
>
> For with the heart one believes unto righteousness, and with the mouth confession is made unto salvation.

Jesus is indispensable because He is our only FOUNDATION.

> Acts 4:11–12
> This is the "stone which was rejected by you builders, which has become the chief cornerstone."

> Nor is there salvation in any other, for there is no other name under heaven given among men by which we must be saved.

Our lives must be built on a Solid Foundation—*Jesus*. He is our base and reason for being. We must build on what Jesus deposits inside us—*the Holy Spirit*.

Jesus is indispensable. He is our only intercessor, our only remedy, our only nourishment, our only source of truth, our only Savior, and our only foundation.

> 2 Corinthians 2:14
> Now thanks *be* to God who always leads us in triumph in Christ, and through us diffuses the fragrance of His knowledge in every place.

We've looked at the amazing things God has provided for us through Jesus. Now, let's take a few minutes to see what God says about therapy.

> Psalm 147:3
> He heals the brokenhearted And binds up their wounds.

> Mark 5:34
> And He said to her, "Daughter, your faith has made you well. Go in peace, and be healed of your affliction."

God's healing is designed for our inner and outer selves. In the first verse listed from Psalms, both the heart (inner) and wounds (outer) are taken care of. When speaking to the woman in Mark, Jesus offers peace (inner) and healing (outer). God's therapy takes care of your whole self. He wants you to be well in your thoughts and feelings and in your actions and physiology. This aligns with

Choice Theory, which is why we're so passionate about bringing you this book.

Through Scripture and the teachings of people like Dr. William Glasser (the developer of Choice Theory), we can live healthy, blessed, and fulfilled lives. It is time we become transformed, utilizing the Word of God. Ultimately, what this means is that we must take a secondary role in our transformation, only to God. We submit to God's leading and then take full responsibility for all our thoughts and actions. We follow God of our own initiative and choose to *not* follow those things that will burden us.

You must be committed to learning, growing, and changing under the leadership of the Holy Spirit. This is our foundation as revealed through Scripture.

> John 15:4–5
> Abide in Me, and I in you. As the branch cannot bear fruit of itself, unless it abides in the vine, neither can you, unless you abide in Me.
>
> I am the vine, you *are* the branches. He who abides in Me, and I in him, bears much fruit; for without Me you can do nothing.
>
> 2 Timothy 2:19
> Nevertheless the solid foundation of God stands, having this seal: "The Lord knows those who are His," and, "Let everyone who names the name of Christ depart from iniquity."

What does yielding to the Spirit of God mean to you?

_____
_____
_____
_____
_____
_____

SCRIPTURE THERAPY AND CHOICE THEORY

What do Godly effective and responsible actions mean to you?

_____
_____
_____
_____
_____
_____

These actions will make you happier and help you gain more effective control of your life, using Scripture as the primary source and then the information from Choice Theory. You will learn to self-motivate, self-evaluate, learn, apply your learning, and determine why and how you behave. This is the development of *spiritual thinking skills*.

Let's forget about *thinking outside the box* and try *thinking through the Spirit of God*.

Explain *thinking through the Spirit of God* in your own words and give a personal example using Scripture to support your response.

_____
_____
_____
_____
_____
_____

Scripture Therapy is about you discovering you, through the Word of God, instead of being the person others want you to be.

Here is an example of what happens when you choose to be the person others want you to be:

> Deuteronomy 30:17–18
> But if your heart turns away so that you do not hear, and are drawn away, and worship other gods and serve them,

> I announce to you today that you shall surely perish; you shall not prolong *your* days in the land which you cross over the Jordan to go in and possess.

God is calling you to decide! *You* choose for yourself how to make changes in your life that will benefit you and the Body of Christ.

> 2 Peter 1:10
> Therefore, brethren, be even more diligent to make your call and election sure, for if you do these things you will never stumble.

When you choose life and health, God's blessings are waiting for you:

> Proverbs 8:19–21
> My fruit *is* better than gold, yes, than fine gold, And my revenue than choice silver.
> I traverse the way of righteousness, In the midst of the paths of justice,
> That I may cause those who love me to inherit wealth, That I may fill their treasuries.

An important part of *Scripture Therapy* is learning and then teaching others. Do your best for God!

> 2 Timothy 2:1–6
> You therefore, my son, be strong in the grace that is in Christ Jesus.
> And the things that you have heard from me among many witnesses, commit these to faithful men who will be able to teach others also.
> You therefore must endure hardship as a good soldier of Jesus Christ.

No one engaged in warfare entangles himself with the affairs of *this* life, that he may please him who enlisted him as a soldier.

And also if anyone competes in athletics, he is not crowned unless he competes according to the rules.

The hard-working farmer must be first to partake of the crops.

2 Timothy 3:16
All Scripture *is* given by inspiration of God, and *is* profitable for doctrine, for reproof, for correction, for instruction in righteousness.

Deuteronomy 4:5–6
Surely I have taught you statutes and judgments, just as the Lord my God commanded me, that you should act according *to them* in the land which you go to possess.

Therefore be careful to observe *them;* for this *is* your wisdom and your understanding in the sight of the peoples who will hear all these statutes, and say, "Surely this great nation *is* a wise and understanding people."

Romans 12:1–2
I beseech you therefore, brethren, by the mercies of God, that you present your bodies a living sacrifice, holy, acceptable to God, *which is* your reasonable service.

And do not be conformed to this world, but be transformed by the renewing of your mind, that you may prove what *is* that good and acceptable and perfect will of God.

Your success in this study is based upon the efforts you put into it. What you do with this information is your choice according to God's free-will plan. If you work through the exercises, self-assess, and make new choices; you will gain a greater understanding of yourself and become the person you desire to be.

CHAPTER 4

Choice Theory and Internal Empowerment

Choice Theory is an internal control psychology that explains how and why we make the choices that determine the course of our lives. It was developed by William Glasser MD and is used extensively in our teaching and counseling. Choice Theory is empowering and life-changing. *Internal* control comes from within and is the power of the Holy Spirit working in us. In contrast, *external* control psychology suggests that it is the things outside of us that cause our behaviors, which is akin to the law of sin and death—bonds that control us.

> Romans 8:2
> For the law of the Spirit of life in Christ Jesus has made me free from the law of sin and death.

In Choice Theory, it is key to understand that everyone has the freedom to choose everything about themselves. And everyone makes their choices in an attempt to meet five basic needs (more about this in the next chapter). Of course, it's a bit more complex than this. But the important starting point is this concept of choice. Many people have grown up believing that they do not have choices or that their choices are limited. They believe that others "make" them do/say/react and that their circumstances force them to behave in certain ways. They often use blaming, criticizing, and complaining when thinking about their life. These people tend to feel powerless and struggle to meet their goals in life. They feel pain and frustration because their needs aren't being met and they can't seem to get others to fix things for them. They rarely experience fulfilling relationships, and conflict is frequent and unresolved.

This is not God's plan for us! God has created us to be free and to experience a full and satisfying life with Him and those around us.

> Galatians 5:1
> Stand fast therefore in the liberty by which Christ has made us free, and do not be entangled again with a yoke of bondage.
>
> 2 Corinthians 3:17
> Now the Lord is the Spirit; and where the Spirit of the Lord *is*, there *is* liberty.
>
> Romans 8:1–2
> *There is* therefore now no condemnation to those who are in Christ Jesus, who do not walk according to the flesh, but according to the Spirit.
>
> For the law of the Spirit of life in Christ Jesus has made me free from the law of sin and death.

Another way to understand Choice Theory is to think in terms of motivation. Our motivation (or reasons) for thinking, speaking, acting, and feeling are all internal. That is they come from within us. This is in direct contrast to reward/punishment theories that say that everything we do is to get rewards or avoid punishment. Choice Theory recognizes the power of the individual to control and change their own life because each action, word, and thought is an individual choice.

You are free to make every choice about your life. Whether these choices are beneficial or not, they are still your choices. Choices you

SCRIPTURE THERAPY AND CHOICE THEORY

made in the past were made to serve some purpose—to try to meet a need. Sinful choices must be acknowledged and sincerely repented for. But that's all. In faith, as well as in Choice Theory, the past does not condemn our present and our future. Choice Theory does not focus at all on the past beyond recognizing that past choices were our best attempt at the time to meet a need.

Our choices right now are focused on relationships and needs *right now*. The past cannot be changed so the past must not be the focus. It may be a challenge at first to focus on the present. Many of us have learned to dwell in the past, reviewing and reliving the pain. But this isn't necessary and can be very harmful. Forget about the suggestion that you can't move forward unless you spend countless hours and resources "working through" your past with a professional. Instead, let's focus on today and learn thoughts and actions that will bring hope and fulfillment to our lives! You can't fix or change the past. But you can have better days starting right now.

In partnership with this concept of personal choice is the removal of responsibility for other people's choices. This can be difficult for Christians. We care deeply about those around us, both for their current situations and their eternal destinations. However, we must focus and become accountable for ourselves and our choices. We cannot control those around us, nor should we!

The Bible and Choice Theory both speak strongly against the practice of working to please others. Again, this can be difficult for Christians. We're taught to love one another and to spur one another on to Godliness, *but* pleasing men is not in our mandate.

> 1 Thessalonians 2:4
> But as we have been approved by God to be entrusted with the gospel, even so we speak, not as pleasing men, but God who tests our hearts.

> Ephesians 6:6
> Not with eyeservice, as men-pleasers, but as bondservants of Christ, doing the will of God from the heart.

BISHOP LES AND SCRIPTURE THERAPY
MINISTER ROXANNE TRICHÉ

This practice of only pleasing God is very liberating. We are not bound to the whims of those around us, and we do not need to spend our energy pleasing people. Dr. William Glasser says, "To achieve and maintain the relationships we need, we must stop choosing to coerce, force, compel, punish, reward, manipulate, boss, motivate, criticize, blame, complain, nag, badger, rank, rate, and withdraw. We must replace these destructive behaviors with choosing to care, listen, support, negotiate, encourage, love, befriend, trust, accept, welcome, and esteem" (*Choice Theory* [HarperCollins, 1998], p. 21).

We challenge you to open your mind to this concept. God has called us to build good relationships with those around us. He has not called us to control them, excuse them, or in any way take away their own freedom of choice.

From your perspective, what is Choice Theory? Find a Scripture that best supports your response and explain why you selected this Scripture.

_____
_____
_____
_____
_____
_____

Perfecting and equipping is about Jesus and *you*! Not your family, not your friends, not your boss, not your image.

Determine if you are allowing others to *play you like a piano*, instead of allowing God to shape you for His purpose.

_____
_____
_____
_____
_____
_____

SCRIPTURE THERAPY AND CHOICE THEORY

If you discover someone in your life is *playing you like a piano*, how can you change this? If you determine you are not being *played like a piano*, how did you avoid this?

_____
_____
_____
_____
_____
_____

Now let's look at internal empowerment.

An important part of the courses we teach is focusing on the process of internal empowerment. Although Christians are used to focusing on the eternal, we are going to focus on the internal here—with eternal results! The internal is where our life is based. It is the thoughts, beliefs, and feelings that translate into the external actions and words we use every day. In Romans, Paul talks about being "transformed by the renewing of your mind." This is not a passive process. It's an active process that requires conscious, intentional choices. We've seen over and over the power of choices in changing the internal—in the renewing of the mind.

Internal is

- existing inside of the body;
- belonging to or existing within the mind;
- within, hidden, unseen.

Internal empowerment is a journey of learning who you are, why you do what you do, how to choose valuable thoughts, how to choose what you want, and then how you make goals to get what you want. Done within the context of Scripture, this process creates confident, healthy, productive followers of Christ.

As you'll learn in chapter 8, God wants us to have goals and dreams that become a reality and lead to joy, fulfillment, and self-empowerment. Self-empowerment is the result of internal empowerment. It's like the destination, and internal empowerment is the journey toward this destination. Internal empowerment coaching teaches individuals to take control over their own lives, establish meaningful and Godly relationships, and operate in the full calling of God in their lives. It's an amazing process, and one we are honored to walk along with you.

> Ephesians 4:4–6
> *There is* one body and one Spirit, just as you were called in one hope of your calling;
> > one Lord, one faith, one baptism;
> > one God and Father of all, who *is* above all, and through all, and in you and in you all.

Another version reads,

> You were all called to travel on the same road and in the same direction, so stay together, both outwardly and inwardly. You have one Master, one faith, one baptism, one God and Father of all, who rules over all, works through all, and is present in all. Everything you are and think and do is permeated with Oneness. (Ephesians 4:4-6 [MSG], Eugene H. Peterson, *The Message*, https://www.biblegateway.com/passage/?search=Ephesians+4%3A4-6&version=MSG)

> 2 Corinthians 4:16
> Therefore we do not lose heart. Even though our outward *man* is perishing, yet the inward man is being renewed day by day.

> Ephesians 3:16
> That He would grant you, according to the riches of His glory, to be strengthened with might through His Spirit in the inner man.

SCRIPTURE THERAPY AND CHOICE THEORY

In your own words, what is *internal?* Find a Scripture that best supports your response and explain why you selected this Scripture.

___
___
___
___
___
___

Empowerment is

- the knowledge and capacity to make one's own decisions.
- the process of gaining knowledge and capacity, and becoming confident in one's own decisions.

Empowerment does not mean becoming someone other than yourself. It does not mean that an introverted person must now blast out the Gospel or that someone must work against their personality and desires to meet some establishment image of what a Christian should be. Empowerment is knowing yourself, understanding your gifts, and being free to make the choices that honor God's call upon your life, and the person He created you to be.

> 1 Corinthians 4:20
> For the kingdom of God *is* not in word but in power.
>
> Proverbs 16:3
> Commit your works to the Lord, And your thoughts will be established.
>
> Philippians 4:13
> I can do all things through Christ who strengthens me.

BISHOP LES AND SCRIPTURE THERAPY
MINISTER ROXANNE TRICHÉ

Luke 24:49–50

"Behold, I send the Promise of My Father upon you; but tarry in the city of Jerusalem until you are endued with power from on high."

And He led them out as far as Bethany, and He lifted up His hands and blessed them.

What does empowerment mean to you, and what has been your personal experience with empowerment? Find a Scripture that best supports your response and explain why you selected this Scripture.

_____
_____
_____
_____
_____
_____

Coaching is

- to instruct, direct, or prompt;
- training intensively.

What does coaching mean to you, and what has been your experience with coaching? Find a Scripture that best supports your response and explain why you selected this Scripture.

_____
_____
_____
_____
_____
_____

SCRIPTURE THERAPY AND CHOICE THEORY

What does God say about coaching?

_____
_____
_____
_____
_____

> 1 Kings 22:5
> Also Jehoshaphat said to the king of Israel, "Please inquire for the word of the Lord today."
>
> Psalm 73:24
> You will guide me with Your counsel And afterward receive me *to* glory.
>
> John 14:26
> "But the Helper, the Holy Spirit, whom the Father will send in My name, He will teach you all things, and bring to your remembrance all things that I said to you."

Internal empowerment is a very individual process. The focus is on meeting the needs that are unique to you, exactly the way God created you. If you've been struggling to become someone others expect you to be, it's no wonder you're experiencing pain and frustration. Others may pressure you to fit their expectations, but the course of your life is up to you. *You* are the only one who knows the desires God has put in your heart. *You* are the only one who knows what your needs, hopes, and dreams are. *You* do not need others to fix your life or make things better. Now is the time to take charge of your life, create meaningful relationships, and enjoy life to the fullest. Let's continue this exciting journey!

CHAPTER 5

Basic Needs

We all have the same five basic needs: survival, love and belonging, power, freedom, and fun. Survival is a physiological need; the other four basic needs are all psychological. These needs drive our Total Behavior (thinking, acting, feeling, and psychology).

You can probably think of someone close to you who has a high need for love and belonging and someone else who has a high need for power. This is what makes us unique—the different strengths of our needs. As you work through this book, you'll understand more about your own needs and their strengths. This will help you better understand why you do the things you do and how to make different choices that will change your life and help you fulfill God's calling in your life.

How you satisfy your needs is your choice, but is it consistent with the Word of God? As you learn about the basic needs, you will begin to understand how and why you behave, and will be able to implement changes according to the Word of God to increase your happiness and ability to engage in effective and responsible actions.

Basic Need 1: Survival

The first basic need is survival. Survival is the desire to be alive and to have a home, food, warmth, security, safety, clothing, rest, sex, and health. This is the deepest and earliest need. This need manifests as urges generated from the brain stem and cerebellum (our "primitive" brain) that cause us to behave in ways that will satisfy our physiological needs.

For most people, survival needs are easily met and do not require much attention. It is easy to forget that the way you satisfy these needs can have an enormous effect on your functioning and behavior. When you do not get adequate rest, food, water, or are not healthy, your body will tell you that something is amiss. If you refuse to listen to these signals, they will become stronger and stronger, resulting in irritability or unhappiness. It is critical to pay attention to your survival needs so you can stay in effective control of your life.

Scripturally, survival and the need for life is represented in the following passages:

> John 3:16
> For God so loved the world that He gave His only begotten Son, that whoever believes in Him should not perish but have everlasting life.

> John 10:10
> The thief does not come except to steal, and to kill, and to destroy. I have come that they may have life, and that they may have *it* more abundantly.

If you do not understand, accept, and apply the principles of these Scriptures, you are not meeting your need for survival. Instead, you are appearing in a realm that leads to being within the reach of death. At birth, you operated in survival mode. If you had a need that was not being met, you cried. It is natural, but it did not take you long to figure out that when you cried, people came running with a bottle in one hand, a diaper in the other, and a blanket under their chin.

So, you learned that when you had a need, you could get it met. You cried to get what you wanted, *or* you learned that if you smiled real cute or pouted your lips, you might get what you want. If some of those behaviors did not work, you learned how to manipulate and express anger to control others—to get what you wanted or what you thought you wanted, even before you were six months old.

As you grew older, if your behavior was not put in check, if you did not learn healthier, more responsible, and more effective behaviors, you continued to manipulate and show anger. This kind of living is not only mentally and emotionally depleting, it will also cause spiritual death.

When manipulating, becoming angry, or other learned behaviors did not work for you, you looked for other ways to get what you want. You learned to try whatever it takes. This could include sex, drugs, stealing, etc., and was all done with little thought—you were in the habit of using any method that might temporarily meet your needs.

When Jesus comes into the picture, you realize a way out of your self-destructive lifestyle. Now when you want something, the Holy Spirit tugs you toward better choices. In addition, adding *Scripture Therapy* and thinking through the Spirit provides an opportunity for making effective and responsible choices. We learn to live life as God intended for us to live it, free from the encumbrances of sinful and noneffective behaviors. Learning to think in a different way will help you get what you want while you fulfill God's calling in your life.

What was also placed inside you before you were born is a deep need to relate to your Savior. When you don't have a true connection to your Savior, your flesh (mind) searches for other ways to fill this need. Thus self-defeating behaviors begin.

It is time you start taking charge of your life and choosing the behaviors that will most effectively meet your needs.

List all the ways you satisfy your survival need. Do not judge yourself here or avoid the truth. Just honestly write how you have been trying to satisfy this need.

_____
_____
_____
_____
_____
_____

How can you improve the ways you meet your need for survival?

_____
_____
_____
_____
_____
_____

Quote a Scripture that best describes survival.

_____
_____
_____
_____
_____
_____

Basic Need 2: Love and Belonging

Love and belonging is the first of the basic needs that is a psychological need. This means it is generated by your "new" brain (the more advanced frontal lobes and areas that control the complex thoughts about yourself). Love and belonging reflects your need for relationships with those around you. You have a genetic need for socialization and interaction. You cannot live a happy life without healthy relationships based on connection.

This need is different from the other needs because you cannot meet it without the involvement of other people. Therefore it is often considered the most difficult need to satisfy. Problems in the areas of love and belonging are often the reason you seek help in your life. Most, if not all, visits to counselors and therapists are because of unmet relationship needs.

People may try to control others in a misguided attempt to meet this need. It will not work! Think of someone who wants friendship but is struggling. They may be in a group of people and choose to pull back and cry. This can initially create a connection to others, but it will not create meaningful, lasting connections. It is an attempt to create relationships using control of others and is not effective. Instead, to meet this need, people must cooperate with, care for, and love others rather than coercing, manipulating, or pressuring them.

One of our students shared her experience in the area of love and belonging:

One student shared that she grew up in a non-Christian home. She was taught how to be independent, have good manners, and take care of herself. By ten years old, she was cooking family meals, and keeping a clean house, and adults praised her for her abilities. She took this praise (associating it with love and belonging) because the feelings were so good she wanted more. She grew up overachieving in search of more love and belonging and learned that hard work didn't feel as good anymore. She became tired, always working for praise.

Driven by her feelings, she decided to become smarter than others. On the outside, she looked like she had it all together; but inside, her feelings were left unchecked—her inner maturity never growing, just her intellect. She felt she was smarter and superior, but overachieving didn't get her the fulfillment in relationships she wanted, so she sought power instead.

She moved into high management, and in the beginning, her need for power appeared to be met. But she soon learned that good was not good enough. Power left unchecked becomes controlling, overbearing, and arrogant.

She pushed people away, and her love and belonging suffered. Since she had always thought with her feelings, she had not developed a clear way of thinking. Now she was looking for yet another way to have her needs met.

She turned to going out after work for cocktails, which felt good at the time. But now her freedom is being stolen by alcohol. She's an alcoholic, losing jobs, pushing people away, feeling herself through life.

There is so much more to this student's life, but she wanted to illustrate how the basic needs should be met in healthy, effective, and responsible ways, instead of the ways she unsuccessfully tried to meet her needs. She emphasized if we let our *thinking* (mind of Christ) do the driving in our lives, instead of our fleshly feelings, we can have more fulfilling and positive end results.

In the space below list all the ways you satisfy your need for love and belonging.

_____
_____
_____
_____
_____
_____

How can you improve the ways you meet your need for love and belonging?

_____
_____
_____
_____
_____
_____

List the most significant Bible verse that represents to you what God says about love and belonging. Then write the status of your love and belonging based upon the Scripture you selected.

_____
_____
_____
_____
_____

Of course, love and belonging requires at least *two* people. Each person's needs are unique. To create healthy relationships, both people should be clear about what they need, and then negotiate so the needs of both people are met.

Basic Need 3: Power

Power is a basic need specific to humans. Certain animals may have all the other four basic needs, but power is a human concept. Power is a very important need to most people, and it includes achievements, feeling important or worthwhile, respect, and having influence over others. The overwhelming need for power has driven our species to extremes, both positive and negative. Power is responsible for the feeling that we need more, even when we have enough.

In *Scripture Therapy*, power is transformed from a force that can take over lives and destroy everything and everyone that stands in its way to a source that comes from within, the *Holy Spirit*. Power is seen not as power over, but internal power.

This definition may seem strange at first. Perhaps you were taught from a young age that to get what you want, you must overpower others. Others may have been taught that power is ungodly. However, with practice and effort, you can live a much happier life by changing the way you use power. It is possible to live a satisfying, influential, productive life without controlling others through the misuse of your personal power.

SCRIPTURE THERAPY AND CHOICE THEORY

Even parents can learn how to raise their children without using external control or exerting their power. This method of parenting will establish strong relationships and teach the next generation to rely on what is inside of them without trying to get what they want at the expense of others.

If power is a strong need for you, your goal can be to increase the power in your life without decreasing the power of another. This is absolutely possible. Power is not limited—to have more or less power does not need to cause someone in your life to have a converse amount of power. Each of us can increase our internal power through the Holy Spirit.

Scripture shows us that God's power is for His followers.

> Isaiah 40:29
> He gives power to the weak, And to *those who have* no might He increases strength.

> Colossians 1:10–12
> That you may walk worthy of the Lord, fully pleasing *Him,* being fruitful in every good work and increasing in the knowledge of God;
>
> strengthened with all might, according to His glorious power, for all patience and longsuffering with joy;
>
> giving thanks to the Father who has qualified us to be partakers of the inheritance of the saints in the light.

Describe God's power.

_____
_____
_____
_____
_____

List all the ways you satisfy your need for power.

_____
_____
_____
_____
_____

Are you using power to control people? If so, how will you choose to change this?

_____
_____
_____
_____
_____
_____

How can you improve the ways you meet your need for Godly power?

_____
_____
_____
_____
_____

Basic Need 4: Freedom

Discovering that you are internally motivated and able to choose your behavior is the key to freedom. Most of us grew up believing others make us act. When you use *Scripture Therapy*, you access the ability to be truly free from external control of any kind.

Freedom is the force for creativity and exploration. It's the desire for independence and having your own space and personal boundaries. It enables you to develop into a unique, independent individual. Loss of freedom causes loss of creativity.

SCRIPTURE THERAPY AND CHOICE THEORY

Often, you don't recognize the importance of freedom until you are deprived of it. When you feel trapped and denied freedom, you will choose a behavior to try to free yourself from whatever is holding you captive.

This need for freedom has given man the strength to overcome many obstacles and challenges throughout the course of history. Freedom also acts as the antidote to external control. People may attempt to force their will on those around them, but the primal need for freedom will push back to avoid being controlled. In *Scripture Therapy*, you discover your freedom comes from within and cannot be taken away by anyone without your consent.

This knowledge allows you to act with free will, rather than reacting to perceived threats to your freedom. We are free to meet our needs in any way we choose. But to protect our relationships and share the love of Christ, we must do this in ways that do not stop others from meeting *their* needs.

List all the ways you satisfy your need for freedom.

_____
_____
_____
_____
_____
_____

List biblical verses stating what God says about meeting your need for freedom.

_____
_____
_____
_____
_____
_____

ity world, be prepared to share this with a few of the most significant people in your life and ask them about their quality worlds. Always listen without judgment, correction, or suggestion. Understanding what each other is seeking in life helps you understand each other better and be more supportive in seeking those things that each person values so highly.

In your relationships, remember that you make every choice about what you think, say, and do. Indirectly, you also choose how you feel about the other person. This applies to every relationship—healthy or not. Although it can feel like your responses feed off others, those responses begin as choices. It takes time and focus to change words and actions when you've become used to reacting in certain ways. But it is completely possible, and when you are aware of the ineffective choices you've been making, you can then choose to make better choices.

Your words and actions are entirely your own, so take responsibility for them. At the same time, the words and actions of the people you care about are *not* your responsibility. (You'll continue to hear this theme throughout the book!) If your spouse or friend is blaming you for what they do and say, refuse to accept the blame. Over time, this is freeing for both of you as you learn to take full responsibility for yourself and are not burdened with blame for another person's choices.

In every relationship, you can only control yourself. Of course, many of us have become used to trying to control those around us, but this is not useful, helpful; nor is it God's plan for us. If you find yourself tempted to control others, ask for God's guidance and strength and choose to give up this control. You'll quickly find that letting go of controlling others improves your relationships, decreases your stress responses, and increases your energy and feeling of well-being.

Choice theory is entirely about the present, not the past. Not to say that the past doesn't matter in life. It certainly does. But the past is unchangeable. It is what it is. All you can do is make choices today about what you will do now. If a relationship is not meeting your needs today, there is no benefit in spending time dragging through what's happened in the past. There is also no benefit in condemning yourself for choices you've made in the past. Those choices were your best attempt at the time to meet your needs, based upon the information you had and the circumstances that existed. Whether they were effective or not doesn't change what happened. Nothing you do now can undo or change the past.

So, you have today to make choices. Think about what you *can* choose. And then make that choice and move forward. You can work to make the relationships you are in right now better, or you can work on creating new relationships. The choice is yours. If the people around you are also seeking better love and relationships, you can share this information with them and journey together. Whether you work together on the relationship or not, you still get to make the choices today for you. As you proceed, continue making choices that work; and when you see that a choice is not beneficial, you get to change and choose something new.

You can also use Choice Theory to improve your relationship with your children. Dr. Glasser's advice about parenting is that if you want your child to grow up to be happy, successful, and close to you, you should not do anything that will cause unnecessary barriers between you and your child.

With parenting, as with all relationships, you choose how you will respond. Problems with children are not uncommon, but each of us is only in control of ourselves. Of course, when our children are young, we must take actions to keep them safe. But as they grow, we have less and less control in their lives. The most important thing is to keep our relationship with them close.

Make sure that your children know your love for them is an undeniable fact that is not connected to whether they do or do not behave in the ways you want them to. Give them the freedom to make choices and learn from those choices. There are things you may need to enforce. But generally, these are far fewer than what most parents believe.

Teach them Choice Theory so they can be free to be who God has made them. Help them know that they get to choose what they do and say—the people around them do not have this control unless it is given. Empower them to choose good thoughts and to find healthy ways to meet their needs.

If there are teenagers in your life, using Choice Theory is the best strategy for maintaining a healthy relationship with them—or creating a relationship where one has been missing. Empower your teens by teaching them that they are in control of themselves. And then let them have control! They are trying to meet their five basic needs just like you are, but they have the added challenges of hormonal changes, confusing peer relationships, and the constant bombardment of social media. The more they realize that their choices are *theirs*, the better they will be able to cope with their life and create the future they want.

The teen years are an excellent time to learn about choices and consequences. Allow them as many choices as possible about their schooling, their clothing, and their hobbies and activities. Be supportive without being controlling or manipulative. The most important part of living with teens is your relationship with them. You can only control yourself—your words, your actions, and by extension, your feelings. Make sure they hear often the message of your love, and make sure this message is not tied to what they do or do not do.

Teens need someone in their life they can trust and connect with. Every parent wants to be this person in their teen's life, but this is not within your control. Be available to your teen, and be open to making sure they have someone they can connect with, even when this someone isn't you. Look for people your teen can have positive relationships with. Their need for love and belonging may not always come from their parents, but it will always be a need they must meet.

There is always something you can *do*, some action you can take in each relationship in your life. Focus on this instead of the other person. This is at the heart of Choice Theory.

SCRIPTURE THERAPY AND CHOICE THEORY

What will you *do today* in a relationship in your life?
_____
_____
_____
_____
_____

It is important to understand the relationship between needs and wants within the five basic needs. Here is an example of one individual's needs and wants:

NEEDS vs. WANTS	NEEDS	WANTS
SURVIVAL	Food, shelter, safety, reproducing	Eat at only five-star restaurants, live in a large house by the beach in a gated community
LOVE AND BELONGING	Family, friends, feeling wanted and needed	Gorgeous, sexy, physically fit partner, great smile, makes me feel special, owns own place
POWER	Success, accomplishments	Make a six-figure income
FREEDOM	Ability to choose, not to be controlled	not to be tied down, able to do what, where and when I want
FUN	Enjoyment, learning, playing	Skiing, boating, travel

BISHOP LES AND SCRIPTURE THERAPY
MINISTER ROXANNE TRICHÉ

Please complete the below chart to help you identify God's needs and wants for you. If you're not sure about something, go ahead and write it down. Then, ask God for wisdom and discernment and review your answers. Trust the Holy Spirit to help you understand what you need and want.

NEEDS VS. WANTS	NEEDS	WANTS
SURVIVAL		
LOVE AND BELONGING		
POWER		
FREEDOM		
FUN		

Dr. Alvin Peterson developed an exercise called *Pete's Pathogram* that has been modified by the authors and encompasses each of the five basic needs. This questionnaire is a quick way to assess your individual needs, time investing in inquiring needs, and level of success in achieving needs.

Complete each item listed in the column below, marking your needs on a scale of 1 to 9—1 being the lowest rating and 9 being the highest rating. Rate each column listed based upon your state of mind at this precise moment.

For example, in the Survival column, rate your perceived need for survival using the above scale. Now, using the same scale, rate the amount of time you invest in obtaining survival. Finally, rate your level of success in achieving the survival you identified in the perceived need section.

SCRIPTURE THERAPY AND CHOICE THEORY

There are no wrong answers. This is strictly a personal reflection on your needs and personality.

Pete's Pathogram

Legend:
- Perceived Need
- Time Invested
- Success Achieved

5 Basic Needs

Instructions
Shade in up to the appropriate number for *each* of the Five Basic Needs

SURVIVAL	LOVE & BELONGING	POWER	FREEDOM	FUN
a desire to be alive, a place to live, food, warmth, security, and safety	friendship, caring, involvement, relationships	success, recognition, respect, accomplishment, being heard	choice, independence, liberty, autonomy, "free will"	discovery, laughing, enjoyment, pleasure, learning, using knowledge

Dr. Arlin V. Peterson (as modified by Les Triche)

Did the results of the *Pete's Pathogram* exercise surprise you? Why or why not?

_____
_____
_____
_____
_____
_____

BISHOP LES AND SCRIPTURE THERAPY
MINISTER ROXANNE TRICHÉ

Now that you have a better understanding of your perceived needs, what can you change to better meet these needs?

_____
_____
_____
_____
_____
_____

CHAPTER 6

SEEAL Assessment

An important part of *Scripture Therapy* is understanding your needs and creating an effective plan to honor God and meet your needs. This chapter looks at the resources you have and the resources you need to grow, change, and fulfill the desires of your heart.

The SEEAL Assessment exercise takes an inventory of where you are today in each of these five areas:

- *S*piritual
- *E*ducation
- *E*conomic
- *A*dministrative
- *L*eadership

Please take advantage of this opportunity for honest self-assessment. Remember, the results of this exercise will be determined by the effort you choose to put into it.

Look carefully at each set of pictures. Select the best picture to represent where you are today. Explain your reasoning.

BISHOP LES AND SCRIPTURE THERAPY
MINISTER ROXANNE TRICHÉ

Spiritual

SCRIPTURE THERAPY AND CHOICE THEORY

What picture did you select? How does that picture represent your spiritual life today?

Is this the picture you want in your life? If not, which picture represents what you want in your spiritual life? Explain.

Education

SCRIPTURE THERAPY AND CHOICE THEORY

What picture did you select? How does that picture represent your educational life today?

_____
_____
_____
_____
_____
_____
_____
_____
_____
_____
_____
_____
_____

Is this the picture you want in your life? If not, which picture represents what you want in your educational life? Explain.

_____
_____
_____
_____
_____
_____
_____
_____
_____
_____
_____
_____
_____

Economic

What picture did you select? How does that picture represent your economic life today?

Is this the picture you want in your life? If not, which picture represents what you want in your economic life? Explain.

BISHOP LES AND SCRIPTURE THERAPY
MINISTER ROXANNE TRICHÉ

Administrative

SCRIPTURE THERAPY AND CHOICE THEORY

What picture did you select? How does that picture represent your administrative life today?

Is this the picture you want in your life? If not, which picture represents what you want in your administrative life? Explain.

BISHOP LES AND SCRIPTURE THERAPY
MINISTER ROXANNE TRICHÉ

Leadership

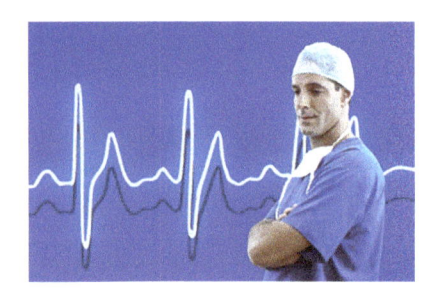

SCRIPTURE THERAPY AND CHOICE THEORY

What picture did you select? How does that picture represent your leadership life today?

Is this the picture you want in your life? If not, which picture represents what you want in your leadership life? Explain.

How far are you from where you want to be in each of the above areas?

Which of these areas in your life needs the most attention? Explain.

What is one change you can make in that area to improve your life?

What did you learn from this exercise?

CHAPTER 7

Your Quality World

You have certain experiences that you value more than others, for instance, specific relationships, certain ideas and beliefs, and things. You have pictures in your mind of these experiences that satisfy one or more of your five basic needs, leading to ultimate happiness. In Choice Theory language, these images make up your quality world. This is an important part of Choice Theory.

Your quality world is as much about what is in it as it is about what is *not* in it. You may have experiences in your past that were very unpleasant or disappointing. This may lead you to *not* have images in your quality world that others would always want in their quality world.

Our country's president might have a much different quality world than a physical therapist living in the same city. Someone might have extreme sports in their quality world, whereas another may have a peaceful spot by a gentle stream in their quality world.

Quality world is also influenced by the culture we live in. The quality world for someone from a third world country will be quite different from someone who lives in a developed nation, even though both have the same five basic needs. A quality world will also be different for people in different stages in their life.

Within your quality world, there are three types of images:

1. People you most want to be with
2. Possessions or things you value most
3. Ideas, beliefs, or preferences for activities you enjoy most

This quality world is our ideal, our perfect destination, or our perfect escape. Ironically, most of us are not consciously aware of our quality world, even though we are constantly comparing our real-life experiences with the images in our quality world. When our experiences match our quality world pictures, we experience happiness. When our experiences don't live up to our quality world, we experience disappointment or frustration.

Occasionally, we will remove someone/something from our quality world when we understand that it can't be acquired. If we replace this with a more accessible picture, we may be happy. We can always add to or take away from our quality world if we choose. But since most people aren't aware of their quality world, they tend to always strive to meet desires and ideals they don't quite understand.

Advertisers are constantly trying to fit their product into your quality world. If they can find the right spokesperson, image, or fantasy, and link it to your quality world, you are far more likely to use your resources on their products as you attempt to have the life that is so important to you.

We also adjust our perceptions of reality to fit our quality world. If we dream of having a child with exceptional musical talent, we may see talent in them when others do not. If a quality world includes working as a teacher because both parents were teachers, someone may pursue this goal relentlessly, regardless of whether they enjoy teaching. If our quality world includes having a spouse, we may choose to stay in a relationship that's abusive rather than risk losing the relationship and being divorced.

Your quality world has a strong impact on your choices, your ideas, your relationships, and your life. It is a crucial part of your life, and it is different from every other person's quality world. You can change things in your quality world. You cannot change things in the quality world of anyone around you. According to Dr. Glasser, "The one thing no one can take away from you is the freedom to control your own Quality World" (*Choice Theory*, p. 55).

It's critical to remember that your quality world is *your* life. Be careful not to assume that others have the same pictures in their quality world. Each individual is unique in what their quality world is made of.

What does Scripture say about your quality world pictures in reference to the people you have in it?

_____
_____
_____
_____
_____

What does Scripture say about your quality world pictures in reference to things?

_____
_____
_____
_____
_____

What does Scripture say about your quality world pictures in reference to beliefs and ideas?

_____
_____
_____
_____
_____

Your quality world pictures do not have to actually exist; they can simply represent images you desire. (Be careful when your desires are not that of the will of God.) Pleasure or happiness results from having experiences similar to pictures in your quality world. The quality world is a source of many of your thoughts and daydreams throughout the day. It is a place you create, to experience a taste of heaven.

> Proverbs 13:11–13
> Wealth *gained by* dishonesty will be diminished,
> But he who gathers by labor will increase.
> Hope deferred makes the heart sick,
> But *when* the desire comes, *it is* a tree of life.
> He who despises the word will be destroyed,
> But he who fears the commandment will be rewarded.

What do your quality world pictures look like? Include relationships/people, things, beliefs and ideas, and values in your description.
_____
_____
_____
_____
_____
_____

What words do you believe express quality world pictures God has for you?
_____
_____
_____
_____
_____
_____

In the following table, list seven or more quality world pictures you can identify.

SCRIPTURE THERAPY AND CHOICE THEORY

My Quality World

People	Beliefs	Things

BISHOP LES AND SCRIPTURE THERAPY
MINISTER ROXANNE TRICHÉ

Look at the list you created. Are there any pictures you are unable to satisfy? If so, what are they?

___

Are there any quality world pictures you think God may want you to replace? If so, what are they? How would your life be happier without these pictures?

___

Most people do not realize they have a quality world, nor are they aware of what's in it. Having an awareness of the pictures in your quality world will provide important clues to help you realize why you experience some of the frustration and pain in your life. The more quality world pictures you satisfy, the happier you will be. This means it may be time to let go of some of the pictures that no longer work for you.

Name at least two Scriptures that confirm your quality world pictures. Explain why and how you choose them.

___

SCRIPTURE THERAPY AND CHOICE THEORY

Recognize that some of your quality world pictures are more important than others and the strength of those pictures depends on the number of needs they satisfy. The more needs that are satisfied by a quality world experience, the more precedence it takes in your life, and the more often you make choices that lead to satisfying that image.

CHAPTER 8
Aligning Your Quality World

Choice Theory teaches that our happiness is determined by the balance between what we have and what we want. Unhappiness is caused when what we have and what we want do not match. This leads to frustration and the feeling of being out of control. The ability to create experiences that match our quality world pictures leads to happiness and the feeling of being in effective control of our lives.

Look back at the My Quality World table you created in chapter 7. What on your list is most likely to be difficult to access, leading to frustration? What does God say about frustration and how you should deal with it?

_____
_____
_____
_____
_____
_____

Is there something else you could use to replace it that will result in getting what God has for you?

Are your actions to get what you want within the boundaries of Godly behaviors? Explain.

We must not sacrifice our Godly character to get what we want. Our character is one of the biggest things God wants. It's our witness to the world of who we are, and what we are all about. It's God who lifts us up. Don't lose sight of that.

What is God's character?

BISHOP LES AND SCRIPTURE THERAPY MINISTER ROXANNE TRICHÉ

How does God's characteristics relate to where you are today?

_____
_____
_____
_____
_____

Your quality world is developed by the experiences you have had since infancy. Images of your parents or caregivers are the first to enter your quality world. Parents and caregivers often share their belief systems, interests, favorite activities, and valued possessions with you, and the associated images are usually reflected in your quality world. As you grow older, you begin developing your own images and start replacing some of the images you had previously.

You have unique life experiences. When you have trouble getting along with another person, it may be because your quality worlds are very different. Your opinions, values, goals, and aspirations are hopefully associated with the people, places, things that God wants you exposed to, and the beliefs you value most. This is what shapes your reality. Other people have their own definitions of reality based on the experiences they have had.

When there is a significant difference between your quality world and that of another person, you usually do not place that person into your quality world. It may be there are parts of your quality world that would match up perfectly, but they are not given a chance to be discovered when your first impressions are of mismatched quality worlds.

Every now and again, you meet a person; and right away, you hit it off. There is an inexplicable something that makes you feel good about being with this person. Once you understand the concept of the quality world, you will realize there is significant overlap between your quality worlds. However, sometimes you don't take time to discover if an overlap is present. You may receive a first impression that highlights your differences and believe that you have

SCRIPTURE THERAPY AND CHOICE THEORY

nothing in common. You may not discover the commonalities unless you intentionally go looking for them. To get along better, it would be beneficial to learn what is in the other person's quality world that you can support.

Think about your current relationship with God. Does your quality world match God's quality world? Explain.

_____
_____
_____
_____
_____
_____
_____

In the diagram below, write in the elements of your quality world that you share (us) and the elements that are separate (God and you), using the words you previously listed that express quality world pictures for you.

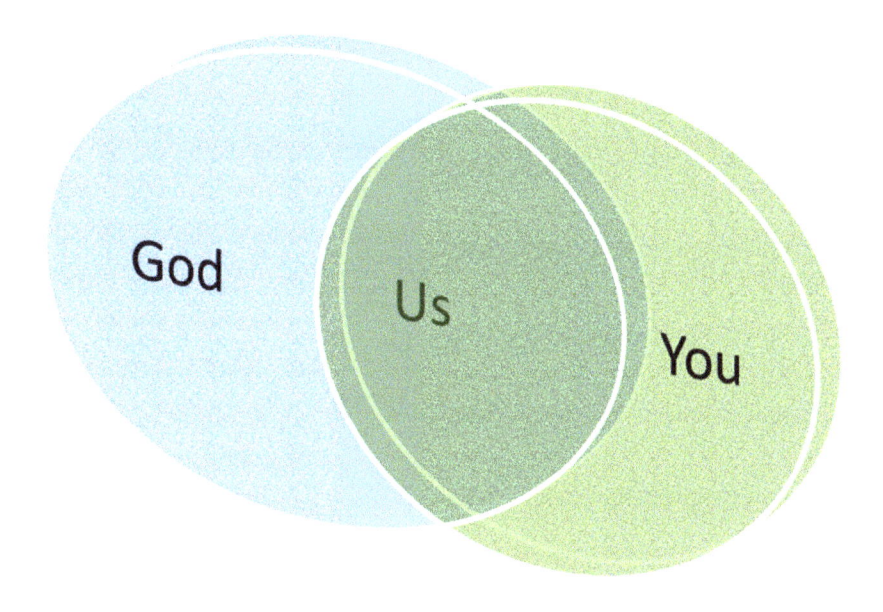

In what way has the quality world concept helped you understand your relationship with God?

_____
_____
_____
_____
_____

Are there pictures in your quality world that need to be removed? What can you replace them with that aligns with God's will for your life?

_____
_____
_____
_____
_____

When you know what the pictures are in your quality world, and you've aligned them with God's will for your life, you can take steps to meet these needs. One step is to choose to use your resources for the things that matter to you. You may be in the habit of focusing time and energy on other people's priorities. Now that you've clarified your own priorities, you can make new choices.

Use your resources for what is in line with your quality world. This isn't selfish, it's smart living. You've aligned the pictures in your quality world with God's will; now you get to make them happen and fulfill God's calling on your life.

SCRIPTURE THERAPY AND CHOICE THEORY

Are there things you are doing that don't fit in your quality world? If there are, how can you stop using your resources on them?

_____
_____
_____
_____
_____

Think about how you can use your strengths. What are you good at that fits with your quality world? How can you include this?

_____
_____
_____
_____
_____

CHAPTER 9

Total Behavior

You generally think of behavior as the way we act or do things. In Choice Theory, this definition is too narrow and avoids the complete responsibility you have in your life. Instead, the term *total behavior* is used. Total behavior includes not only your actions but also your thoughts, your feelings, and your physiology. Physiology includes all your body responses that relate to your behaviors—things like your heart beating faster, your palms sweating, and your breathing becoming shallow when you are scared.

You are most conscious of your control over your actions and thoughts. However, changing actions and thoughts lead to changing feelings and physiology. This is how you are responsible for total behavior in your life. No, you can't directly change how you feel. But you can direct your thoughts and actions toward specific needs, which in turn changes your feelings and many aspects of your physiology.

An important aspect of total behavior is understanding that you're always trying to make the best choice for the time you are in. This doesn't mean the choice is good; it just means you're using what you think is the best method to meet a need. Choice Theory doesn't deal with the past, except to remember that past choices were best attempts at the time. There's no need for guilt, incrimination, or rehashing the past. Instead, the focus is on actions now and choices now. You either benefit from effective and responsible choices or suffer from ineffective and irresponsible choices.

SCRIPTURE THERAPY AND CHOICE THEORY

Total behavior is always seeking to achieve the pictures from your quality world. When it works, you choose to feel happy and fulfilled. When it doesn't work, you choose to feel unhappy and frustrated. When you are choosing a behavior that is causing pain, you have three choices for change. You can either change what you want (your quality world picture), change what you are doing (your total behavior), or change both.

You don't *have* to do anything when your total behavior is not meeting your needs or is causing pain; doing nothing is still a choice that is yours to make. But if you feel stuck and you want to feel better, try asking yourself, "What am I going to do today?" Make a choice and take an action and then evaluate how effective it was. You can always keep on doing what you're doing or make a different choice and try something else.

Understanding total behavior leads to an exceptional level of personal freedom. You are not constrained by misery, circumstances, people, or any other influence. You choose your thoughts and actions. Freedom enters every aspect of your life when you realize that you are in control of your total behavior.

An inspiring example from Scripture is the time when David danced to the Lord. His celebration of the return of the ark of the Lord was a personal statement of the joy he was feeling, and he danced unrestrained and "with all his might" (2 Sam. 6:12–15). We can imagine his thoughts, we can see his actions, and we can feel his exuberance. The criticism and disdain that Michal, daughter of Saul, tried to place on him had no effect on his total behavior. David's response showed his freedom from worry over the judgment of others and his freedom to express himself before the Lord without restraint. Many of us dream of living and worshipping with such freedom.

It's challenging to change when you're used to letting circumstances dictate your feelings. You can begin by focusing on your actions. Instead of analyzing how you feel when you wake up, ask yourself, "What am I going to *do* today?"

BISHOP LES AND SCRIPTURE THERAPY
MINISTER ROXANNE TRICHÉ

John 13:17
If you know these things, blessed are you if you do them.

What is keeping you from "dancing to the Lord," as David did, and taking charge of your life?

_____
_____
_____
_____
_____
_____

You are now being asked to step away from people, situations, and things you *allow* to control and define who you are and cause you to become distracted from your Godly call and assignments.

Are there people, situations, and things you need to step away from? If so, what are they?

_____
_____
_____
_____
_____
_____

Now you can use the total behavior model and apply it to every part of your life! Let's use happiness as an example. Scripture is full of verses about happiness and joy:

Luke 1:14
And you will have joy and gladness, and many will rejoice at his birth.

SCRIPTURE THERAPY AND CHOICE THEORY

> Psalm 16:11
> You will show me the path of life; In Your presence *is* fullness of joy; At Your right hand *are* pleasures forevermore.

But many Christians are *not* living with joy and happiness. If you are feeling the same way, there are things you can do today to begin experiencing happiness. Start with your thoughts. Are you focusing on things that bring sadness and worry? You can refocus your thoughts on effective and responsible things. Remember this verse:

> Philippians 4:8
> Finally, brethren, whatever things are true, whatever things *are* noble, whatever things *are* just, whatever things *are* pure, whatever things *are* lovely, whatever things *are* of good report, if *there is* any virtue and if *there is* anything praiseworthy—meditate on these things.

It's the combination of these quality thoughts that brings happiness. It may be true that you are deeply in debt, but since it is not lovely, of good report, and praiseworthy, don't fix your thoughts on it. If you are continually slipping into negative thoughts or memories, you must practice thinking good thoughts instead. It may be something as simple as repeating "God loves me" to yourself to start. Focus on that thought bringing healing and joy. Add more thoughts as you are able.

You may need to pay attention to thoughts you choose to think about others. Remember that in Choice Theory, you control only yourself. There is no benefit in thinking about how you wish others would change or how much someone hurt you or what you wish you'd said during an argument or anything else that involves complaining, criticizing, controlling, manipulating, or agonizing.

Whenever you realize your thoughts are not in line with Philippians 4:8, stop yourself and begin repeating the good thoughts instead. You become what you think.

> Proverbs 23:7
> For as he thinks in his heart, so *is* he. "Eat and drink!" he says to you, But his heart is not with you.

If you want to enjoy feeling happy, think good thoughts.

What are some good thoughts that are worth meditating on?
_____
_____
_____
_____
_____
_____

Happiness also comes when we release ourselves from trying to make others happy. Just as you are fully responsible for your thoughts, actions, feelings, and behaviors, you are *not* responsible for other people's thoughts, actions, feelings, and behaviors. This is another challenge for Christians who deeply care about those around them. But when you substitute caring for controlling, you put your own happiness and freedom at risk. Remind yourself often that the actions of others are not your responsibility.

> Galatians 6:4–5
> But let each one examine his own work, and then he will have rejoicing in himself alone, and not in another.
> For each one shall bear his own load.

If we aren't accountable for other people's actions before God, then there's no value in trying to control people here on earth. You are not responsible for the actions of your children, your spouse, your neighbor, or the ladies group at church.

As you change your thoughts, change your words and actions. Encourage this process by speaking thoughtfully. Instead of criticizing, blaming, or complaining, try listening, loving, and supporting. You have control over what you say, but you may need to change some of the ways you have gotten used to speaking. Instead of reacting to others, work on choosing your words.

Communicating—the words and actions we use to give information to others—is an important part of total behavior and of our Christian walk. Choice Theory includes some important lessons in communicating. For those people you are closest to, sharing your quality world with them and learning of their quality world is important. You've consciously aligned your quality world with God's calling in your life.

Now it's time to share it with the people you care about. They can join you in these goals—or maybe they won't—but you can give them the information. In the same way, take the time to learn what's in their quality world. Maybe you've never asked what your teen wants in their life or even what your spouse wants. Find out and look for ways to support them.

As you communicate with others, remember that *you* are in control of *you*. You don't need to brace yourself against a possible slight or negative message. Listen to what other people are saying and choose to accept only the information that is true and helpful. If it's not, let it go. You can focus your mind on worthy thoughts as you remember who you are.

You do not need anyone else to fix you or make you feel better. When you receive empowering and encouraging information, accept it graciously. But don't wait for someone to fix your life. You have access to all the choices you need to make to get on a good path and move toward the things in your quality world. Seek healthy relationships and useful truth and refuse to accept lies and condemnation.

Remembering that you are not responsible for the total behavior of other people will also help you communicate better. You're not under any pressure to fix the people you're talking to, or change them. There's no controlling agenda in healthy communication. This allows you to communicate in a relaxed, nonthreatening way and will often open doors that seemed to be closed. Continue to focus on the one thing you are responsible for—you—and your communication with everyone will benefit.

Finally, give yourself permission to have fun! Get out there and laugh a little! Don't worry if you're out of practice—God has created you to experience joy and happiness. The potential for happiness is within all of us.

CHAPTER 10

PRITTT Formula

An important part of Spiritual Therapy is understanding your needs and resources. We've already discussed the five basic needs from Choice Theory (survival, love and belonging, power, freedom, and fun). Now, let's look at some of the more practical components you need, using the PRITTT Formula. Here's how it breaks down:

*P*eople to assist you and serve as your personal board of directors
*R*esources and opportunities to gather information
*I*dentification of relevant facts and information
*T*echnology, tools, and supplies, and a plan for their acquisition
*T*alents, new skills, and character traits for achieving success
*T*ime + cost estimates of how long it will take and the potential loss of time, money, and effort

We'll cover each of these areas in more detail, but here's an example of how a student responded to this exercise:

My plan is to give back to others by helping them achieve and maintain happiness.

People: *Personal board of directors, family, mentors, anyone who wants help others become happier.*

Resources: *Studying the Bible and learning what God says about happiness.*

Information: *Scripture Therapy and Choice Theory application for becoming happier, and eliminating external control in one's life.*

Technology: *A laptop or tablet and Internet, to have access to e-books related to happiness.*

Talents: *Hear the voice of God with clarity; have compassion, patience, discernment, discipline, research skills.*

Time + Cost: *This is a lifelong goal, I will continue to sharpen my skills and receive certification as a Scripture Therapy Minster within two years. This goal will cost me old habits, the loss of friends, and some family who may want me to live in the past, instead of pursuing God.*

Now let's look at each section.

People to Assist You and Serve as Your Personal Board of Directors

We understand and accept the value of seeking advice, and we tend to do this. Even the act of reading this book is a choice to seek counsel. The Bible has many verses about seeking counsel, accepting discipline, and the quest for instruction.

Proverbs 15:22–23
Without counsel, plans go awry, But in the multitude of counselors they are established.
A man has joy by the answer of his mouth, And a word *spoken* in due season, how good *it is!*

SCRIPTURE THERAPY AND CHOICE THEORY

Proverbs 12:15
The way of a fool *is* right in his own eyes, But he who heeds counsel *is* wise.

Proverbs 19:20
Listen to counsel and receive instruction, That you may be wise in your latter days.

Matthew 7:7–8
Ask, and it will be given to you; seek, and you will find; knock, and it will be opened to you.
For everyone who asks receives, and he who seeks finds, and to him who knocks it will be opened.

A personal board of directors is an important aspect of your growth and progress and follows the biblical guidance of seeking counsel. This is not necessarily a formal group where members know each other but rather a group of individuals of your choice that you connect with regularly. These are people that know more than you in different areas or can offer alternative views than you are likely to see. They're people you will ask for advice and feedback. They are a group of individuals charged with providing insight, time, direction, and resources to enable the leader (chairperson/you) to obtain your vision, goals, objectives, and help you get what God wants you to have and keep you accountable.

Creating your personal board of directors is different from finding a mentor. The directors may not be older than you or more experienced than you or even in your field of work. Rather, it's a group of experts in different areas that each contribute something valuable to your life.

As you consider who to include, think of people you already ask for advice. It will be your job to approach them, both to ask if they'll participate and to continue to engage with them. Look for people willing to give you honest answers, even when it's not what you want to hear. These will probably not be close friends. Include people that offer diversity and perspectives that will challenge your thinking. You don't want someone who will always go along with what you say without questioning or challenging you.

Look for the following types of people to include in your personal board of directors. If you only know of one or two right now, start with them and then ask who else they would recommend. Always choose people you respect:

1. Someone who can offer reliable financial advice.
2. Someone who can cut through the fog to deliver honest evaluations.
3. Someone who is from (and connected to) a younger generation.
4. Someone who is more advanced than you.
5. Someone who thrives on making connections.
6. Someone who is a forward and productive thinker.

When you have identified someone you'd like to include, talk to them when you both have some available time, and neither one of you will be rushed. Tell them you are looking for a personal board of directors—a group of people you can occasionally access individually for advice and insight. Let the individual know what you would appreciate receiving from them (a balanced perspective, insight into financial decisions, etc.).

Be sure to connect with each of them once in a while (at least every few months). This will depend on your goal(s) and how involved you are with them, even just to share where you are in your life goals. Ask for thirty minutes of their time over coffee, Skype, or however you most effectively communicate with them. Remember, your personal board of directors can include people from out of state or another country. Always thank them for their time and effort. When you've used their advice, let them know and tell them how it has helped you and brought you closer to, or helped you achieve, a goal.

Describe how you think a personal board of directors can help you obtain your vision, goals, and objectives and help you get closer to what God wants you to have.

_____
_____
_____
_____
_____

List the people you would like on your personal board of directors, along with how and when you will contact them to ask for their help.

_____
_____
_____
_____
_____

Resources and Opportunities to Gather Information

You already have resources and experiences that can help you meet your goals. Think back over your life. Are there times when you survived against the odds? Have you worked through nearly impossible situations and circumstances? Have you taken courses, training, or had the opportunity to learn new things because of interactions with different types of people? These are all resources you can now draw on.

What and who are your resources?

_____
_____
_____
_____
_____

Identification of Relevant Facts and Information

You need to know what you need to know! It's important to clarify what information you will need to accomplish your life goals. This can include training, courses, and work experience.

What information do you need?

_____
_____
_____
_____
_____

Technology, Tools, and Supplies, and a Plan for Their Acquisition

What physical things will you need? An office? A vehicle? A computer? Will you need a one-time purchase of supplies or regular purchases? How will you get these things? If you're unsure, pray for creativity to acquire the things you need and write down ideas and answers as they come to you, or it may be appropriate to ask the advice of your personal board of directors.

What technology do you need?

_____
_____
_____
_____
_____

Talents, New Skills, and Character Traits for Achieving Success

This takes a bit of introspection, especially when it comes to your character. It may be easy to identify the talents and new skills you need, but what character traits will you need? There may be some obvious ones, like patience for those working with children. But you may need to add to your list as you keep these needs in mind. It can help if you imagine yourself actively involved in your goal and write down the traits you see yourself using.

What talents, skills, and character traits do you need to succeed?
_____
_____
_____
_____
_____
_____

Time + Cost Estimates of How Long It Will Take and the Potential Loss of Time, Money, and Effort

What will it cost you in time, resources, and sacrifices to meet your goals? Some may say it would cost them friends and family members who weren't supportive. It's important to be realistic. There is often a price to be paid.

What will your life goals cost you?
_____
_____
_____
_____
_____
_____

BISHOP LES AND SCRIPTURE THERAPY
MINISTER ROXANNE TRICHÉ

Now, take a minute to summarize, in one sentence per item, your PRITTT+Cost formula analysis:

P _____
R _____
I _____
T _____
T _____
T+ Cost _____

CHAPTER 11

Giving Back and Mentoring

There's no question that giving is part of God's plan for us. But in this, as in all things, it is your choice. It is important to hear what the Spirit has to say when considering this choice—not only when to give but what and how to give. Giving can involve money, time, talents, things, blessings, and love. Let's look at some Scriptures about giving:

> Deuteronomy 15:10
> You shall surely give to him, and your heart should not be grieved when you give to him, because for this thing the Lord your God will bless you in all your works and in all to which you put your hand.

> 2 Corinthians 9:6–11
> But this *I say:* He who sows sparingly will also reap sparingly, and he who sows bountifully will also reap bountifully.
> *So let* each one *give* as he purposes in his heart, not grudgingly or of necessity; for God loves a cheerful giver.
> And God *is* able to make all grace abound toward you, that you, always having all suffi-

ciency in all *things,* may have an abundance for every good work.

As it is written: "He has dispersed abroad, He has given to the poor; His righteousness endures forever."

Now may He who supplies seed to the sower, and bread for food, supply and multiply the seed you have *sown* and increase the fruits of your righteousness, while *you are* enriched in everything for all liberality, which causes thanksgiving through us to God.

The verses above from 2 Corinthians encompass everything about giving: the principle of sowing and reaping, the choices and feelings of the giver, the giving through actions ("every good work"), the ability to have more to give ("increase the fruits of your righteousness"), and freedom ("liberality") that comes from giving.

If giving has not been in your quality world until now, consider adding it. Giving is good, rewarding, freeing, and joyful. As images come to you, write down how giving looks in your quality world pictures.

Let's backtrack a minute and think of total behavior and how it relates to giving.

What are your thoughts about giving?

_____
_____
_____
_____
_____
_____

SCRIPTURE THERAPY AND CHOICE THEORY

What are your feelings toward giving?

Are these thoughts and feelings aligned with Scripture? If not, what choices can you make to change this?

What are your current giving actions?

Are these the actions you want to take? Explain.

What exactly do you want to do to give back?
_____
_____
_____
_____
_____

Now, let's look specifically at mentoring. Mentoring is a type of giving where you offer your support, advice, and encouragement to a willing individual to help them meet their goals. It can mean sharing the lessons you've learned that help you in life, challenging an individual to excel in their talents, teaching someone a trade, and much, much more.

> Proverbs 27:17
> *As* iron sharpens iron, So a man sharpens the countenance of his friend.

> 1 Peter 5:2–4
> Shepherd the flock of God which is among you, serving as overseers, not by compulsion but willingly, not for dishonest gain but eagerly;
> > nor as being lords over those entrusted to you, but being examples to the flock;
> > and when the Chief Shepherd appears, you will receive the crown of glory that does not fade away.

SCRIPTURE THERAPY AND CHOICE THEORY

What do you offer as a mentor? What have you learned that you would like to share with others?

As stated in 1 Peter 5:3, how can you mentor without trying to control those you mentor?

Is there someone you can mentor now? If not, how can you create opportunities to meet people who you can be available to mentor?

If you are a business owner, manager, supervisor, or have authority over a group or individuals, you can use the principles of Choice Theory in your leadership role. These principles will enhance relationships, benefit your bottom line, and empower those you connect with as if you are in a mentoring capacity.

In the same way that you found freedom through the understanding that you only control yourself, you can empower your employees to find this same freedom. In this capacity, your job is to help your employees identify and activate the power within themselves.

Create an environment where growth and development are encouraged within the workplace. Ask what they want to learn and how they want to develop their careers. Provide opportunities where they can gain training and move forward.

Encourage employees to self-evaluate and create plans and goals beneficial to their careers. Find out what employment pictures are in their quality worlds and have them make plans to meet these needs. Have a method for employees to share these goals in a nonthreatening environment and take suitable actions to promote these suggestions. Often, employees have the best ideas for operating in more efficient and productive ways—they just need to be able to share them.

When employees see their workplace instituting their ideas, it reinforces their value to the company and fosters an atmosphere of teamwork and mutual goals. This also increases the commitment employees feel to their employer. They can go from seeing their job as just a paycheck to feeling like an important contributor to the workplace. This leads to lower turnover, fewer sick days, and more productive employees.

Give employees as much power as possible within their positions to make changes, take full responsibility for their work, and contribute to operations beyond their immediate tasks. Listen to them in the breakroom, on the job, and through their evaluations. For some employees, the relationship they have with their manager is one of the closest relationships in their life. Use these opportunities to provide a positive influence and to encourage these people in their lives.

Remember that there are other pictures in their quality worlds that they are seeking, and keep an open mind to the ways the workplace can be flexible so employees can have as many needs satisfied as possible. Be willing to change. If you realize there's a better way to do something, set the example and change. Don't hang on to meaningless policies or inflexible rules. Instead, shift policies and rules to benefit the needs of your employees and institute their suggestions.

SCRIPTURE THERAPY AND CHOICE THEORY

The result will be confident, productive, creative employees who are committed to their job.

In his book *Choice Theory*, Dr. Glasser even claims, "A good workplace, in which you have some power and work for people who don't try to push you around, is very good for your marriage" (p. 98). The way you interact with your employees can have a long-reaching positive impact on their lives.

If you have responsibility for others, how can you provide mentorship and empowerment?

CHAPTER 12

Self-Change through Self-Evaluation

It is helpful to self-examine by responding to the following questions. Take your time and ask the Spirit of God to reveal to you how to respond and ensure your responses incorporate what God is saying to you.

What does God want me to have?

_____
_____
_____
_____
_____
_____

Specifically, what am I doing to get what God has for me?

_____
_____
_____
_____
_____
_____

SCRIPTURE THERAPY AND CHOICE THEORY

Is what I am doing to get what God has for me working? If not, why?

What are my plans to get what God has for me using effective and responsible means?

Who have I connected with to form a personal board of directors?

How can the PRITTT + Cost model help me get what God has for me?

What is my detailed plan to give back/pay it forward to others using what I learned from this course?

_____
_____
_____
_____
_____

How will I encourage others to become scripturally empowered?

_____
_____
_____
_____
_____

Evaluation and follow-up are an important part of your progress. After you have prayerfully made your plans and taken actions, you should check if what you are doing is working. Are you getting closer to your goals? Are you choosing effective and responsible actions? If you are, continue. If you are not, change as needed. Continue to look on your past choices as your best attempts, at that time, to meet your needs. If they weren't the best choices, don't get caught up in blame or negative self-talk. Just take the information you've learned to make new, more effective plans.

SCRIPTURE THERAPY AND CHOICE THEORY

Let's continue with self-evaluation by answering the following questions:

What has changed in my thoughts since I began this book?
_____
_____
_____
_____
_____

What has changed in my actions (both words and physical actions) since I began this book?
_____
_____
_____
_____
_____

What has changed in my feelings since I began this book?
_____
_____
_____
_____
_____

What has changed in my physiology (physical symptoms and signs) since I began this book?
_____
_____
_____
_____
_____

BISHOP LES AND SCRIPTURE THERAPY
MINISTER ROXANNE TRICHÉ

What have I removed from my quality world?

What have I added to or changed in my quality world?

Am I meeting more of my needs or less of my needs? If more, what is working? If less, what have I tried that is not working?

What am I going to do now? Include things you will keep doing, things you will stop doing, and things you will start doing, but keep it simple and clear.

SCRIPTURE THERAPY AND CHOICE THEORY

What are my thoughts about the future?

_____
_____
_____
_____
_____
_____

What are my feelings for the future?

_____
_____
_____
_____
_____
_____

While reading this book, what Scriptures have had the most impact on you?

_____
_____
_____
_____
_____
_____

CHAPTER 13
Reflecting and Summary

Scripture Therapy has introduced you to an ongoing process of knowing Scripture, hearing and obeying God, and making and evaluating choices in your life. The principles you've learned will always apply to your life if you choose.

At the beginning of the book, you answered some questions about yourself—who are you? Go back and read through those. Has anything changed since you wrote these? It is an accurate reflection of who you are now? Explain.

_____
_____
_____
_____
_____
_____

Scripture is always available. It guides us in cultivating good relationships, choosing effective behavior, and making life-changing choices. It is the power of our indescribable God. Scripture reminds us that Jesus is our only intercessor, our only remedy, our only nourishment, our only source of truth, our only Savior, and our only foundation.

For most people, this is the first time they've learned about Choice Theory. Because it's so different from what we've all been taught, it can take time to sink in. It's the opposite of external control psychology that suggests all behavior results from external forces such as the chance to earn a reward or avoid punishment. Instead, Choice Theory explains that our total behavior is motivated from within—from the choices we make in attempts to meet our needs.

God has given each of us choices. Choices about what we think, what we say, what we do, and by extension what we feel both emotionally and physically. We all get to choose right now what our next behavior will be. We don't get to choose for others. Each person's choices are their own. We only answer to God for our own choices, not the choices of others. As part of this journey, you know you are free from trying to make others do or say anything. All you can do is give them information and embrace the choices you make.

Choice Theory does not focus on the past since nothing about the past can be changed. This doesn't mean you ignore your past, but it does mean you cannot blame your choices today on your past. Although this also can take time to get used to, it's incredibly liberating. God has freed you from the bonds of your past, and you are free today because of this.

Everything you choose in your life is for the purpose of meeting your five basic needs of survival, love and belonging, power, freedom, and fun. While everyone shares these same needs, the strengths of the needs are different for everyone, and this is part of our uniqueness. You have ideas or pictures in mind of what it looks like when these needs are met. These pictures are known as your quality world and include people, things, ideas, and beliefs that are the most valuable to you. The more these pictures are realized in your life, the happier and more fulfilled you will feel. When these needs are not met, or they seem out of reach, you feel pain and frustration.

Throughout this book, you've been looking at your own needs and your quality world. Take a few minutes to sum up what you need most.

_____
_____
_____
_____
_____

Write down some of the things in your quality world.

_____
_____
_____
_____
_____

These needs and desires will remain out of your reach without a plan. You've taken the time to write a PRITTT+Cost formula analysis of the people, resources, and traits you need. Review those here.

P _____
R _____
I _____
T _____
T _____
T _____

Congratulations! You've begun a journey of freedom, choices, opportunities, and fulfilling God's calling in your life. Every day, you will wake up with a fresh chance to choose how you will behave in every way to everyone. This process is fluid and open to change and adaptation as you meet needs and desires and grow and change.

God bless you in your life!

Scripture Therapy and Choice Theory® Glossary of Terms

The definitions in this document are from *Scripture Therapy*, Choice Theory, and Internal Empowerment manuals, or they are self-generated definitions based upon common use.

Terms

Ability. The power or skill to do something.

Achieve. To get or reach a goal by working hard to become successful.

Acting wheel. On our car of life, acting is the right front wheel of behavior. Acting is the component of total behavior that we have the most control over, as it is our choice to do something.

Aggressive. Characterized by or tending toward unprovoked offensives, attacks, invasions, or the like.

Author. A person who writes a novel, poem, essay, or the like; the composer of a literary work.

Basic needs. We all have the same five basic needs to live (survival), to love and belong, to have power or self-esteem, to be free to make choices (freedom), and to have fun.

Behavior. Internal empowerment coaching expands the single word *behavior* to two words *Total behavior*. *Total* because it always consists of the four components: acting, thinking, feeling, and the physiology associated with all our actions, thoughts, and feelings. All behaviors are internally motivated, purposeful, flexible, and creative.

Behavioral system. The place where created or known behavior is chosen in our best attempt to balance the comparing place scale and increase our sense of effective control in our lives.

Believe. To accept or regard an idea or concept as true; to accept the truth of what is said by someone; to have a specified opinion.

Belonging. As used in *love and belonging*. One of the five basic needs that drives, inspires, and informs us not only to the point of caring for others who we might not know, but also to seek satisfying relationships with other people.

Blaming. Assigning responsibility to another when something goes wrong. Often used to avoid taking personal responsibility and ownership of our choices.

Caring habits. In Choice Theory, caring habits are supporting, encouraging, listening, accepting, trusting, respecting, and negotiating differences.

Car of life. Our car of life is the way we control our life by the choices we make, which are expressed as total behavior, steering our life down all the roads we choose.

Challenge. A call to engage in any contest of skill, strength, and the like or demand to explain, justify, and the like.

Challenging. Testing one's abilities; demanding.

Character. The way someone thinks, feels, and behaves; someone's personality; a set of qualities that are shared by many people in a group, country, and so forth and make a place or thing different from other places or things.

Choice. The act of picking or deciding between two or more possibilities, the opportunity or power to make a decision, a range of things that can be chosen.

Choice theory. An internal control psychology that explains why and how we make the choices that determine the course of our lives.

Cliff. Critical point or situation beyond, which something bad or undesirable may occur; a very steep, vertical, or overhanging face of rock, earth, or ice.

Comparing place. The place where we become aware that a picture in our quality world is unsatisfied by the tipping of the scale. We compare what we want from our quality world with what we have from our perceived world.

Competence. Having the skills and ability to accomplish a task. It fulfills our basic need for power and contributes to our feelings of well-being.

Complaining. Expressing critical remarks about a person or situation; this is an external control, which negatively affects relationships.

Commitment. A promise to do or give something; a promise to be loyal to someone or something; the attitude of someone who works very hard to do or support something.

Control system loop. Either positive or negative feedback created when one is in effective control of their lives. See also **Situation A**, **Situation B** "How the Brain Works"—situation A for negative feedback or situation B for positive feedback.

Consequence. Something that happens as a result of our own behavior. Consequences are not punishment.

Contribute. To give to help a person, group, cause, or organization; to help to cause something to happen.

Controlling. Having a need to control other people's behavior; having the power or giving someone the power to control how something is managed or done.

Cost. The price of something; something that is lost, damaged, or given up to achieve or get something.

Creativity. The ability to create something new that has never before existed in the life of the creator. Often it will provide the creator with more control over his or her own behavior.

Criticizing. To judge or find fault with something or someone. A form of external control when we believe we know what is right for another.

Crossroads. A place where two or more roads cross; a road that crosses a main road or that runs across land between main roads; a crucial point especially where a decision must be made.

Dangerous. Characterized by danger; able or likely to cause injury, pain, harm, or death.

Deadly habits. In Choice Theory, deadly habits are criticizing, blaming, complaining, nagging, threatening, punishing, bribing, or threatening to control.

Desire. To want something; to express a wish for.

Different. Partly or totally unlike, not the same, not ordinary or common.

Education. The action or process of teaching someone especially in a school, college, or university; the knowledge, skill, and understanding that you get from attending a school, college, or university.

Encouraging. Facilitating hope or promise in a way that connects people and satisfies needs.

Effective. Producing a result that is wanted; having an intended effect.

Effective control. When we are meeting all our five basic needs using effective and responsible behavior.

Endurance. The ability to do something difficult for a long time.

Enhance. To increase or improve something.

Eradicate. To remove something completely; to eliminate or destroy.

Evaluate. To assess the value or condition of someone or something in a careful and thoughtful way.

Excuses. What we say to ourselves and others to try to avoid blame or justify when we do not do something we need to do to get better control of our lives.

Exercise. Physical activity that is done to become stronger and healthier; something that is done or practiced to develop a particular skill.

Explanation. The act or process of making something clear or easy to understand; the act or process of telling, showing, or being the reason for or cause of something.

Explore. To talk, think, or look at something in a thoughtful and detailed way to learn more about it; to learn about something by trying it.

External control. An aggressive method of control that is forced, coerced, imposed, or otherwise generated from outside of ourselves where everyone is harmed, the controllers as much as the controlled. Examples of external control are criticizing, complaining, blaming, nagging, threatening, punishing, bribing, and rewarding to control.

Feelings. A state of mind or often unreasoned opinion or belief; whenever we behave, we are feeling something. Choice Theory teaches that we can learn to control what we feel.

Feeling wheel. A right-rear-wheel behavioral choice on our car of life, which we have little or less control over, like anger or embarrassment.

Forensic. The art or study of formal debate; relating to the use of scientific methods or knowledge in solving crimes; a closely examined look at one's relationships, behaviors, choices, and trust issues.

Freedom. The ability to live life the way we want to live it and achieve our own goals and still get along well with the people we need; the capacity to act without hindrance or restraint; a sense of well-being or peace of mind.

Frustration signal. This signal is felt as an urge to behave.

SCRIPTURE THERAPY AND CHOICE THEORY

Fun. The feeling of enjoyment, pleasure, laughter, and learning in our quality world.

Genetic instructions. The signals that drive our psychological needs.

Goal. The end toward which effort is directed; determining priorities and what is most desirable and less important without infringing on the rights of others.

Growth. Progressive development, evolution, increase, or expansion.

Happiness. A state of well-being and contentment; a pleasurable satisfaction.

Illustrate. To give examples to make easier to understand; to be proof or evidence of; to explain or decorate a story, book, and so forth with pictures.

Immediate. Happening without delay; made or done at once; related to the present time.

-ing. This is used when choosing a behavior (like depress*ing*, anxiety*ing*, guilt*ing*, and so forth) as opposed to suffering from an ailment; an intentional suffix for indicating action.

Increase. To make or become larger or greater in size, amount, number, and so forth

Interpretation. The way something is explained or understood; a particular way of performing something.

Invite. To ask someone to go somewhere; to ask formally or politely to do something.

Journey. An act of traveling from one place to another.

Knowledge. Information, understanding, or skill that you get from experience or education; awareness of something.

Learned. Something that people get or have because of learning or experience.

Love. Commitment; one of the five basic needs used in Choice Theory-Internal Empowerment Coaching as *love and belonging*. For a loving and sexual relationship to last, we need friendship and a life of our own—"not a sexual life, but a social or recreational life, separate from the relationship."

Loving from across the street. Maintain a relationship with another person while at the same time putting physical, emotional, and social distance between oneself and the other person for the purpose of devoting more time to yourself to find happiness, focus on life challenges, and self-evaluate.

Meaningful. Something that matters to us and is part of our total knowledge.

Meeting. An intellectual discussion in which participants discuss their opinions and learn new information; to define, personalize, and challenge oneself and others through specific terms.

Method. A way of doing something; a careful or organized plan that controls the way something is done.

Mindfulness. The practice of maintaining a nonjudgmental state of heightened or complete awareness of one's thoughts, emotions, or experiences on a moment-to-moment basis.

Nagging. To irritate by constant scolding and urging or finding fault; a form of external control, which is not effective.

Need. A situation in which someone or something must do or have something; something that is required to live, succeed, or be happy.

Negative behaviors. Behaviors that do not further Choice Theory principles: criticizing, complaining, blaming, nagging, threatening, punishing, bribing, or rewarding to control.

Negotiating differences. A Choice Theory negotiation occurs when each person involved in a dispute states what he or she is willing to do to resolve the difference. We do not try to make someone else do anything. We can only control our own behavior.

New brain. Where the seat of all conscious and voluntary need satisfying behaviors are located.

Obstacle. Something that makes it difficult to do something; an object that you have to go around or over; something that blocks your path.

Obtain. To gain or get, usually by effort.

Old brain. Our basic need for survival is monitored automatically in this lower area of the brain located in the section that includes the structure below the cerebral cortex.

Opportunity. An amount of time or a situation in which something can be done.

Organized behavior. A way of behaving that is firmly established as a part of our quality world.

Perceived world. The way we see the world. No two perceived worlds can be exactly the same because of the information we each have acquired.

Perceptual camera. An internal device that we use to apply our own beliefs and values on incoming information.

Perceptual system. The place in the "How The Brain Works" chart where information is compared to our total knowledge and given a meaning; it consists of the total knowledge filter and valuing filter.

Perspective. A view of things in their true relationship or relative importance; the state of one's ideas, the facts known to one, and so forth.

Personal board of directors. A body of persons charged with providing insight, time, direction, and resources to enable the student to realize his or her vision, goals, and objectives.

Physiology. The ways that living things or any of their parts function; the way in which our body reacts to information received, for example, sweaty palms, tense muscles, dry mouth, and so forth.

Physiology wheel. Behavior choices on our car of life, which are on the left back wheel and are harder to control such as our blood pressure, heartbeat, and other body signals.

Plan. A set of actions that have been thought of as a way to do or achieve something; something that a person intends to do; something we decide to do to help obtain what we want.

Plant. To put or plant in the ground to grow; to invest in the vision, purpose, or mission.

Positive behaviors. Behaviors that promote a positive atmosphere where Choice Theory thrives: listening, supporting, encouraging, accepting, trusting, respecting, and negotiating differences.

Power. Encompasses recognition, skill, competence, and importance. This does not mean power over someone, but rather where our skills, accomplishments, or beliefs bring power to ourselves. Power is generated from within, like being proud of ourselves and being listened to by others.

Practice. To do something again and again to become better at it; to do regularly or constantly as an ordinary part of life.

Prepare. To make yourself ready for something that you will be doing, something that you expect to happen, and so on; to make or create something so that it is ready for use.

Protect. To keep someone or something from being harmed, lost, or the like.

Prune. To cut off or trim back unwanted parts or individuals who become a distraction to our goal or accomplishments.

Psychological. Of, pertaining to, dealing with, or affecting the mind, especially as a function of awareness, feeling, or motivation.

Psychology. The science or study of the mind and behavior; the way a person or group thinks.

Pursue. To follow and try to catch or capture for usually a long distance or time; to be involved in an activity.

Quality world. All the people, things, ideas, and ideals that we have stored in our belief system that represent what we want most. We experience them as mental pictures associated with strongly positive feelings when satisfied. Awareness of these pictures and their alignment with our behaviors will increase the quality of our lives.

Rate. To decide the importance of something or someone in our lives. This is done on a scale of 1–10 with one being the least, and ten being the most.

Reality therapy. The unique questioning technique associated with the WDEP process (What do you want? What are you doing to get what you want? Is what you are doing working? What is your plan?); it is based on Choice Theory and focuses on improving present relationships, almost always disregarding past relationships. Success depends on creating a good relationship between the client and the counselor.

Reaffirming. Stating again as a fact; assert again strongly.

Reallocate. Reuse resources in a different way.

Recognize. To know and remember because of previous knowledge or experience; to accept or be aware that something is true or exists.

Real world. The world, as it exists, without our distortions or perceptions. This world is impossible for us to see without distortion because our only view of it is through our own sensory perception.

Reflection. An idea or opinion formed as a result of deep thinking; an image that is seen in a mirror or on a shiny surface.

Reframe. To restructure negative life experiences or circumstances for the purpose of yielding positive outcomes; to view or express words or a concept or plan differently.

Relationship. The way in which two or more people, groups, countries, and the like talk to, behave toward, and deal with each other; a romantic or sexual friendship between two people; the way in which two or more people or things are connected.

Resemble. To look or be like someone or something.

Responsible. Having the job or duty of dealing with or taking care of something or someone; able to be trusted to do what is right or to do the things that are expected or required.

Restore. To give back someone or something that was lost or taken; to return someone or something; to put or bring back into existence or use; to return to an earlier or original condition by repairing it, cleaning it, and so forth.

Safe. Not able or likely to be hurt or harmed in any way; not able or likely to be lost, taken away, or given away; not involving or likely to involve danger, harm, or loss.

Satisfy. To cause to be happy or pleased; to provide, do, or have what is desired.

Scripture therapy counseling. The study of Choice Theory and Internal Empowerment Coaching from a biblical perspective, the foundation of "All, and in all," as created by God.

Security. The state of being protected or safe from harm; things done to make people or places safe.

Self-trust. Self-confidence.

Self-evaluation. To carefully study and determine the worth, significance or condition of yourself or some aspect of life; ask yourself whether what you are doing now is going to get you closer to, or farther from, the pictures you hold in your quality world.

Senses. Touch, sight, hearing, taste, and smell.

Sensory system. All our senses make up this system and transmit information from the real world to our brain.

Situation A. We are not in effective control.

Situation B. We are gaining more effective control.

Skill. The ability to do something that comes from training, experience, or practice.

Solution. Something that is used or done to deal with and end a problem; a correct answer or explanation to a problem, puzzle, and the like.

Solving circle. A group of individuals that agree to negotiate differences to reach a satisfactory compromise or resolve an issue.

Story. An account of incidents or events.

Strength. The quality that allows someone to deal with problems in a determined and effective way; the ability to resist being moved or broken by individuals or force.

Survival. Meeting our basic instinctual needs, such as food, fight, or flight; the state or fact of continuing to live or exist especially in spite of difficult conditions; the desire to be alive, a place to live, food, warmth, security, and safety.

Talent. A special ability that allows someone to do something well.

Teaching. Instruction given to increase knowledge; the ideas and beliefs that are taught by a person, religion, and the like.

The bars. Information passing through the sensory system into the total knowledge filter and on into the valuing filter or perceptual system depicted in the "How the Brain Works" chart by different-colored bars, depending on its personal meaning.

SCRIPTURE THERAPY AND CHOICE THEORY

Thinking. The action of using your mind to produce ideas, decisions, memories, and the like.

Thinking wheel. The front-left-wheel behavior choice on our car of life, which we are in control of most of the time, as we have the power to determine what we think.

Timeline. A listing of important events for successive years within a particular historical period.

Total behavior. The four individual components of behavior: acting, thinking, feeling, and physiology.

Total knowledge filter. Consists of everything we have learned and determines if a stimulus is recognized when it enters the brain through the sensory system.

Trusting. Believing what someone says; learning to trust, especially trusting yourself, gives you personal freedom and plays a role in every relationship. Learning who we can trust can be a lifelong process.

Trapped. Caught or confined in a restricted position or place.

Utilize. To use something for a particular purpose.

Utopia. A place where there is complete perfection.

Valuable. Worth a lot, very useful or helpful, important and limited in amount.

Valuing filter. Once input passes the total knowledge filter and has been recognized, the valuing filter assigns it a positive, negative, or neutral value dependent on individual perception.

Vision. The ability to see; sight or eyesight; something that you imagine; a picture that you see in your mind.

Want. To desire or wish for; to want something; to be without something wanted or desired.

Willing. Quick to act or respond; doing something or ready to do something without being persuaded: done, made, or given by choice.

About the Authors

Presiding Bishop Lester Triché is the president and founder of IECAST Inc. He is a senior faculty member with the William Glasser Institute and was trained and certified in Reality Therapy/Choice Theory and Advanced Practicum by the late renowned Dr. William Glasser MD of the William Glasser Institute. Charged by Dr. Glasser to do so, he created the Choice Theory® Connections-Internal Empowerment Coaching Program.

Bishop Triché is a state and community corrections provider, offering leadership and instruction in Choice Theory, Reality Therapy, and *Scripture Therapy* Counseling—the study of why and how we behave. His focus is on facilitating reframing, restoring, and reallocating resources to enhance individuals' relationships, behaviors, choices, and self-trust, through effective and responsible means.

Bishop Triché holds an AA in sociology, a BA in behavioral science with a certificate in criminal justice and corrections, an MA in public administration, an MA in public policy, and a PhD (Honor Causa) in public administration. He has completed all courses for a second doctorate in judicial law and public policy at the Claremont Graduate University. Additionally, Bishop Triché is a graduate of the John Maxwell University as a teacher, coach, and motivational speaker. He has an extensive track record of providing consulting services to corporate boardrooms; invested groups in South America, Mainland China, South Africa, and other countries; as well as to organizations in gang-controlled areas in Los Angeles.

*****

Scripture Therapy Minister RoxAnne Triché is the executive vice president of IECAST Inc. She serves as a master facilitator and has taught internal empowerment coaching and leadership coaching at various correctional institutions on a voluntary basis for the past five years. Additionally, she provides coaching to businesses, leaders, and frontline personnel.

Minister Triché is a certified Internal Empowerment Coach through Loyola Marymount University, Los Angeles, California, and a graduate of the John Maxwell University as a teacher, coach, and motivational speaker. She is Choice Theory/Reality Therapy certified through the William Glasser Institute. She is mentored personally by Carleen Glasser in her monthly practicum.

Minister Triché has also served as a leader and trainer in teamwork and conflict resolution in corporate America for twenty-three years. She consults with corporations and public and private organizations regarding various business, staffing, and management needs. She has hands-on experience in conducting administrative and business audits, policy design, training and professional development, marketing, and legal compliance. She specializes in employee coaching, human resources acquisition, strategic planning, risk management, organizational development, and implementation and assessments.

CPSIA information can be obtained
at www.ICGtesting.com
Printed in the USA
FSHW01n1300140718
50324FS